The Gospel According to Harry

The Gospel According to Harry

Harry MacDonald

Published 2008 by Temple DPS Ltd

Copyright © 2008 Harry MacDonald

The right of Harry MacDonald to be identified as the Author of this Work
has been asserted by him in accordance with the Copyright, Designs and
Patents Act 1988

British Library Cataloguing in Publication Data
A catalogue record for this book is available from the British Library

ISBN: 978-0-9543956-5-0

Print management: Temple Design
www.templedesign.org

Printed and bound by CPI Antony Rowe, Eastbourne

Contents

Plays and musicals written by the author:

A Share of the Action *(musical)*
All on the Losing Side *(musical)*
All in the Mind
Lloyd George Knew My Mother
Three in One
Larry Boy and Viv
20th Century Views *(musical)*
All that Loving Stuff
Don't Call Us, We'll Call You.

Preface to the Gospel according to Harry

A dictionary definition of the word gospel will define the word as glad tidings. It is also defined as the certain and infallible truths of the revelation of the Christian faith as set down in the first four books of the New Testament.

The gospels of my predecessors, Mathew, Mark, Luke and John, however, do not, unfortunately, contain sure and certain infallible truths. The purpose of my gospel is to point out that the whole foundations of Christianity, and indeed, other religions are based on a fallacy.

Jesus was no doubt a good, well-meaning man. It is possible that he genuinely believed that he was the son of the one and only god. His end was cruel and tragic. But our four friends undoubtedly portrayed a much exaggerated version of his life worthy of today's most outrageous and rampant tabloids. And no Press Council on hand to keep them in check.

Did he really walk on water, produce all those loaves and fishes, raise people from the dead, and above all did he really rise from his tomb and ascend into an unknown heaven? The modern world has no knowledge of miracles. Why should they have suddenly stopped 2000 years ago?

The first part of my gospel is to suggest in a light-hearted, but nevertheless rational way how Mankind came into being, how they came to believe in gods and how these beliefs were developed into complex and divisive dogma and strange rites. I have interspersed my comments with autobiographical details of my personal journey through life just to illustrate I'm an ordinary sort of a bloke and not some crackpot.

The second part of my book is to beggar the belief that you cannot become a "good" person unless you have some blind faith in a mythical god. I cannot ever claim to be good but we can have a shot at it. So I have simply put down my views on how to set the world to rights. This is my gift to Mankind. You lucky readers. Enjoy.

H.M.

Part One

1

Adam and Eve and all that

In the beginning there was nothing. Nothing. No thing. Consider the concept of nothingness. Eerie.

Then, as it is writ in the ancient unproven books, God made the earth in six days, pretty good going even though half of it is actually sea, then he made the animals, vegetables and minerals and all the creepy crawlies. Then he switched on the sun so there was light during the day and then he made the stars and the moon which gave a lesser light during the darkness, unless it was cloudy when things go bump in the night, although, unlike today, there wasn't much to bump into.

Next he made Man and called him Adam. And God thought he would be lonely, so he put Adam into a deep sleep, cut out one of his ribs and made it into a female and brought her before Adam and Adam said she would be called Wo-man, because she was taken out of him. Feminists, try not to cringe. And they were both naked and unashamed although nearly all paintings of them show them wearing fig-leaves, one for Adam and three for Eve, that's her name by the way.

And on the seventh day God rested because he'd really had a very hard week, and that is why all the pubs and shops were shut on Sunday until after the end of the Second World War. Except in Wales and Scotland where they held out for a further twenty years.

Then God sent a very devious talking serpent to Adam, who casually asked Adam if it was true that God had said he should not pick apples from the third tree on the right. Fortunately Adam and Eve both happened to speak Serpentese. Eve, who happened to be standing by, immediately said certainly not and instinctively took an apple from one of the trees in question and took a bite from it. Immediately, there was thunder, lightning, sheer bedlam let loose.

Adam was furious with Eve, "Now look what you have done, you've made God angry" and then God himself chipped in and said "And furthermore, because you have committed an original sin, from this day all future generations will have to atone for your sin". Or something like that, there are several versions.

"What!" said Eve. "Just for scrumping one measly apple? But that's alright, go on, blame the woman, it's her fault as usual. This is absolutely ridiculous." And she stamped her foot on a stone which made her even more hopping mad.

"I suppose it is a bit heavy," said Adam grudgingly. "Perhaps it's just supposed to be allegorical," to which Eve probably gave a withering look.

Now is that a likely story? I think not, but there are millions of people who believe every word of it. Well, I may have got some of the details wrong, it may have been the second tree on the left, but I think that's the gist of it.

2

The Big Bang from the Big Brains

So, we're back to nothing again. But nothing is a real problem, there must have been something. One theory goes there was a large dollop of rocks and gases, it is not known how these were formed, but give us a hundred years or so and some of our very clever chaps will crack that. In fact they're working on it right now in some tunnel near Geneva.

Then there was possibly a bang, a big bang. A VERY BIG BANG. BIG TIME BANG.

This lump of whatever it was fragmented then spread out in all directions at a furious rate and is reckoned to be still travelling outwards and still extending our universe. On the way some of these lumps ignited and shed light and became stars. These massive balls of fire attracted smaller lumps of matter which then began to whiz round these stars taking light and warmth from them. These are called planets and we live on a little planet called Earth. Planet Earth is just one of millions of planets going round their respective suns.

So here we are on our little planet going round our sun every twenty-four hours. Every morning we can see our star in the sky, except in Britain where it's usually raining, and on every cloudless night we can see a vast number of these magic little specks of fire which are providing light to their various planets.

There are, of course many learned explanations of the Big Bang theory and you can go on to read the clever chaps if you can. The trouble is you have to have a degree in astronomy and mathematics before you can begin to understand them, but the above is again the gist of it.

It is humbling to contemplate the vastness of the Universe, the apparently unending areas of space and stars which are around us.

But each living creature, humans included, tends to see itself as the very centre of that vast universe. The ants scamper round looking for food; the little mouse wakes up and resumes his life-long search for sustenance; the tiger mercilessly pursues his prey; the human being living in what they call a "developed" country generally eats too much and now borders on obesity. But he still tries to improve his little lot. A person from a poorer country, on the other hand, barely has sufficient to feed himself, the even poorer are at starvation levels. Most humans are trying to improve their conditions, and above all survive in a competitive world.

In short, every animal, human or otherwise is essentially self-centred and self-seeking - in fact just plain selfish. This is the condition which all living beings share. The task for civilisation today is to mutate our behaviour into being less self-centred and demonstrate a greater regard for our fellow human beings. We cannot begin to do this, however, until we get our own lives in order. You know, not all me, me, me. Try and be a nice, useful chap and all that. Some little thing like good manners would be a great start, that is how civilisation started.

Does this sound like Christianity? Not necessarily. Why should Christians claim all the Moral High Ground? More of that later, as Karl Marx said to Adam Smith. For my younger readers, if there are any, they represent the extreme poles of political and economic thinking.

3

From Little Blobs to Big Slobs

So, how did life start on our little planet? Not, I think, with a fully grown Adam and Eve assembled in haste by an entirely fictitious god. The most learned explanation of how life began can be found in Charles Darwin's "Origin of Species". One could spend a lifetime studying and learning from just one chapter of this truly great man's work. Darwin was so astounded by his findings that he could not bring himself to tell his wife about them for over ten years as the lady was a devout Christian and he didn't wish to offend her.

Let me try to remind you of his theory in simple terms.

After the Big Bang, our planet was just a piece of rock and water going round the sun. No life at all, just as there is apparently no life on the other planets in our solar system.

After several million years, no need for hurry, maybe the planet was warming up, or even cooling down. But then things began to happen. On the seashore possibly, or by a muddy pool where it rains a lot, perhaps in the Manchester area or more likely in Equatorial Africa where it is warmer. One day up pops an amoeba, a tiny being of the simplest structure. I would hazard a guess that it made a little glugging noise as it triumphantly raised its little head out of the mud. Very soon this gallant leader was joined by several other amoebas all gluggering about. After several thousand years of this, the amoebas not surprisingly got rather bored. Food was almost non-existent, transport was difficult because these little fellows didn't have any legs, and the view from the mud wasn't too good, so again one really enterprising amoeba decided he would change into a bigger amoeba. With a bigger and more versatile kind of protoplasm, a kind of blob. This process is a known as a Mutation.

Out of this protoplasm one chap decided he would go off to sea and become a fish, another plumped for plant life and became a pea, whilst another less energetic one just slid further into the ground and became a potato.

This is how the favourite dish of the British people became fish, chips and mushy peas.

And so it came to pass that on the 4th day of May in 1925 AD, Henry Jack MacDonald and his wife Jeannie Morgan MacDonald begat their third son at 44, Montgomery Road, Scotstoun, Glasgow and he was named the same as his father. But please, please nobody call me Henry!

During this very exciting period of mass mutations there were some really extraordinary career choices. One can understand a go-ahead type of blob wanting to develop into a noble kind of animal like a horse, or a Ferrari of the jungle like a cheetah, or a leopard with lovely coats and all, or the majestic eagle with its piercing eyes soaring above in the skies. But a giraffe, who would choose to be a giraffe? He must have a difficult job just standing up. That is a very strange choice, as is the Giant Ant Eater with a snout nearly as long as the M1 sniffing up ants all day. But it was all about food availability, and the giraffe is, after all, a very haughty creature who only eats at the top table, whilst most big animals don't want to grub along the ground for ants, so it's all quite logical in a twisted kind of way.

The sheer range and size of the various species, from the almost invisible insect to the lovely old elephant, is truly remarkable. The young human animal would do well to explore this fascinating subject and would probably find it more interesting than some of those tired old science fiction stories. It certainly is true that fact is stranger than fiction.

The world owes a huge debt of gratitude to the prodigious David Attenborough and several other clever chaps whose wildlife films widened our knowledge and understanding of animal and plant life. We all have two things in common: a determination to survive and an equal determination to reproduce our species. That's why the world is full of crying babies and lovely little kittens and puppies, not to mention nasty wasps nests at the bottom of your garden.

Talking about crying babies, six months after I was born my family moved to the small South Welsh port of Barry. My father, who was in shipbuilding, had been appointed manager of Barry Graving Dock. That's a dry dock where ships are repaired, so he had a pretty good job and we were comfortably off at a time of economic hardship. My first memory is looking up from my pram at two ladies talking, one of them was my mother, pretty boring I'm afraid. We lived at 4, St Nicholas Drive, Barry. I attended St. Baruch's Infant School and fell madly in love with Miss Atwell, my teacher.

Being somewhat squeamish, I am sometimes horrified by wildlife scenes where you see graphic shots of a lion chasing and tearing a zebra to bits, or a dolphin getting stuck into a cuddly seal for breakfast. But the law of the jungle is eat or be eaten, or at best eat for a little while and then be eaten, it's a cruel old world. The plants grow to be eaten by sheep and cattle who in turn are eaten by humans, the antelope grazes to be eaten by the lion or the tiger, the bigger fishes eat the smaller fishes whilst the vulture finds a source of nourishment by dining on the remains of the corpses, in fact the world is just one vast food chain.

Apart from the need to feed, the other driving force is to reproduce. Here again we are grateful to those film makers and writers who have described or illustrated the various fascinating ways in which different species mate and reproduce.

The arrogant, rebellious youth of the 1960s challenged the old social order of the day and established a less deferential and more open type of society. Some of this was good; the passage of time has also shown that some of it was not so good. In their arrogance they seem to have implied that they actually invented sexual intercourse. Well, they didn't, but they certainly made the subject less taboo.

So strong is the sexual urge that Sigmund Freud, the accredited founder of psychiatry, proclaimed that everything we do is sexually motivated and any activity is simply a substitute for sexual activity. So, take heart all you stamp-collectors and people who take down train numbers, you are actually making love. But more of that later, as the actress said to the bishop.

About four years later my father got an even better job as Manager of the Mount Stewart Dry Dock in Cardiff. The family moved to 122, Westbourne Road, Penarth.

My eldest brother, Ian, was four years older than me, so he was a slightly remote figure, but there was only

*eighteen months between me and my other brother Jim,
so we became very close. There was a large field opposite
our house, flanked by trees. We called it Jim's field, well
he was more acquisitive than me. We scrumped apples,
climbed trees, vandalised a few allotments, we were just
two typical horrible little kids.*

But to return to the early development of the species.
During the development of the amoeba into embryonic
choice one very bright amoeba must have decided it would
be a good wheeze to be able to climb trees, swing gleefully
along the branches, pick up any nuts or berries that were
going, and for good measure frighten the smaller animals
by jumping on them. This little imp is known as the
monkey. He thrived because of his speed and agility; he also
seemed to be one of the species that enjoyed living,
jumping from tree to tree and squealing with delight.

If you look at some of the other species, many of them
are not really having much fun. The peacock is always
showing off, displaying his fine feathers and preening
himself, the camel has always got the hump, not just
because of the hump on his back but also by his general
demeanour, birds and rabbits always look terrified, frogs
just hop now and again on their spindly legs and do the
odd croak. I always think some dogs, like the St. Bernard
for instance, look really sad, but monkeys actually enjoy
life.

It is good to have such a happy, mischievous ancestor
because soon (well, after a couple of million years or so)
the little monkey was to lose its tail and eventually to
develop into the great ape families from whom sprang your
very own Uncle Fred and Aunt Edna.

This is not really so bad as it might seem at first glance. Several learned men and women have spent months at a time trying to get close to these big fellows. Diane Fossey's brilliant film about her experiences living with the Mountain Gorillas of Africa is particularly enlightening. She found them the most gentle of creatures with an affectionate and structured family life. And they can show care and affection for their fellow creatures. Scientists still speak wistfully of the "Missing Link" between the great apes and Homo Sapiens, which, translated from the Latin means Wise Man. On reflection this seems a rather generous term for modern man with his constant conflicts and squabbles. But it is now almost universally accepted by the scientific world that we are direct descendants of these big chaps. That is why modern man suffers a great deal from backache, because we were originally designed to walk on all fours. Always a good excuse for the odd day off work. Like thousands of people I have suffered from backache and when I consulted my doctor about the complaint he told me the human being still retains the beginning of our monkey's tail at the base of his spine. Which was very interesting but didn't do a lot for my backache.

Gradually, over many years, the apes began to straighten up. First there was Homobentus, then Homonotsobentus, then Homonotquitesobentus, then there was Homo Erectus. After another million years or so came Homo Sapiens. Something had clicked within his (or her) brain which enabled him to communicate by speech, to be able to make tools and implements and to be able to pass on his skills and knowledge to his offspring.

When I was nine years old, my father died. Our lives were soon to be changed for ever. I was much in awe of my father, perhaps even a little afraid. He had been ill for some time, perhaps weighed down with heavy responsibilities in the difficult economic period of the thirties. We had two maids, one was called Daisy, the other one was only fifteen, I don't remember her name but she cried most of the time because she was homesick and was required to live in. We also had a gardener who came in two days a week and a washer-woman who came in on a Monday. If she was in a good mood she let me operate the old-fashioned mangle. Best of all was a chauffeur who was employed by the company but was at our mother's beck and call. Mr Smith had been an officer in the First World War. We referred to him as Smith, what a cheek, but our washer-woman had to be called Mrs Robbins whilst we called our gardener Jim. Such were the mysteries of the British class system. My brothers and I adored Smith, he was so kind and full of fun. I always hoped he prospered later on in his life.

Just before my father died, my mother told me he wanted to see me in his bedroom. I was very nervous at what offence I may have committed. He was dying, although I was not aware of that at the time, and he spoke to me very gently and kindly for a few moments before shaking hands with me and wishing me a good future. Two days before he died I remember my mother very distraught on her knees praying to God to spare him. This puzzled me somewhat as they had spent much of the time shouting at and quarrelling with each other. This memory of their continual conflict tended to make me very apprehensive of the state of marriage in later life.

My father's funeral was a huge affair, as they were in those days. I remember watching what seemed to be an endless procession following the horse-drawn hearse past our house. I felt more than a tinge of pride; sorrow came later, with understanding. Looking back on his life, I was grateful for that last conversation with him.

But I must say that my childhood up to that time had been very happy.

It is reckoned that Mr and Mrs Homo Sapiens are only 150,000 years old but in that time they have been able to construct and then destroy several civilisations, travel the earth by sea and air, build magnificent buildings, indulge in mass slaughter of their fellows, land a man on the moon, create great works of art, music and literature and play silly computer games.

But men and women are still animals. The Twentieth Century was a great time for scientific and industrial progress. It was also a record century for massacres on an unheard of scale. They started in 1906 with the Turks murdering the Armenians, then came the murderous futility of the 1914-18 war, where millions died. In one day in the Battle of the Somme the British suffered 50,000 casualties. In one day! Enough to fill a football stadium. The Germans only lost 49,000 that day so they were proclaimed the winners, although the Allies actually gained a hundred yards of muddy territory, so perhaps it was just a draw. Then the Japanese set about slaughtering the odd million Chinese and thousands of people lost their lives putting down the evil Nazi regimes of Germany and Japan. Then there was the little matter of the slaughter of five (or was it six) million Jews by the descendants of Beethoven, Mozart and Goethe. In the meantime, the Russians had been busy annihilating about 20 million of their citizens with a few thousand Poles thrown in for good measure. We had minor massacres in the Balkans but the century was rounded off by the Rwanda orgy of killings and continues into the 21st Century with the Darfur massacres. How many millions was that?

So do we really need reminding that we are animals?

The point of these previous pages is just to emphasise that we do spring from a common ancestor which is a simple blob of reproductive matter. "We few, we happy few, we band of blobbers" as Shakespeare might have written, if he'd only known.

Some people resent this and deny it in the most vehement way, but all the science says it is true. Not many of us believe nowadays that the Earth is flat, and most of us now accept the unpalatable fact that the world's climate is changing.

The hope is that the human race will eventually accept that we are the children of unpredictable Nature. We should accept that, because of our origins, we are selfish beings. We should also accept that human nature has made some faltering steps to creating a more civilised society, but the journey is only just beginning.

Organised religion, with its misguided belief in redemption or damnation, simply gets in the way of progress. We've just got to become good eggs. Virtue has its own reward, vice its own castigation.

We are not creatures tainted by Original Sin, hoping that if we are good boys and girls we can book our ticket to the next world.

But if we don't believe in any god and we don't believe in a choice between Heaven and Hell, how do we claim the Moral High Ground?

Read on. All will be revealed.

After my father died it soon emerged that my mother had enjoyed the good life. She loved clothes and had a prodigious collection of shoes, but no provision had been made for a rainy day. Consequently my mother was broke. She had been a teacher but was not permitted to teach in Wales because she could not speak Welsh. So we had to sell our house in Penarth and move to Bristol. Times were hard and she found great difficulty in selling the house for which my father had paid £950, a large sum of money in those days. The local Minister of the Church said she mustn't worry as God would sell it. If he did sell it, he got a rotten price, as my mother only received £450 for our lovely home. Did this sow some little seeds in my mind?

Up till that time, my two brothers and I had been to private junior schools. My mother had to turn her attention to our future education. My father had been a Freemason. The Freemasons managed Boarding Schools for sons and daughters of deceased Freemasons. My two brothers were over the age for entry and subsequently attended Colston's School, Bristol, but I was young enough to be eligible for the Royal Masonic Junior School for Boys in Bushey, Hertfordshire.

4

How Primitive Man came to imagine gods

One of the most recent significant discoveries was the discovery of DNA by two clever chaps from Cambridge University, Messrs. Watson and Crick. I am sure the letters DNA stand for something very scientifically significant but fundamentally it is a method of identifying each gene in an animal or plant. A gene is a hereditary factor which has been carried from parent to child and which determines hereditary characteristics.

As a result of these findings it has been discovered that we humans share 92% of our genes with a mouse. As you can imagine the South African Rugby Union team who recently won the World Cup wouldn't like to accept that one little bit. On the other hand we share 91% of our DNA with a lion, so that's better.

There has recently been great interest in the television programme "Who do you think you are?" Because of the wonders of the internet it is now fairly easy to trace back a few generations. My daughter recently phoned me excitedly to inform me that my great-grandfather was a boat builder who lived on the tiny island of Coll, close to the Isle of Mull, part of the Western Isles of Scotland. Bully for him, very interesting, sounds like a good life.

People talk about "good" families, which implies that there are "bad" families. The so-called "good" families come from royalty and what used to be referred to as "the nobility". In fact, the "good" families are probably more illness prone as they are often inter-bred.

Don't worry if you only spring from the common herd, because we all go back to that little blob.

Life was very hard for early man, just as it is now for wildlife and in those scattered parts where primitive tribes eke out a frugal existence, although often a happy one as some intrepid explorers have testified. Life was a constant struggle to get enough to eat and drink, to find shelter, to protect themselves and their offspring from danger, just simply to survive.

Early man soon found that they could hunt and survive more easily if they banded together in groups. This was the hunter-gatherer period where the men hunted and the woman picked berries and looked after the young. After a period they moved on to new hunting grounds where they hoped the pickings and the hunt would be more productive. There are still Nomadic tribes in parts of the world to this day.

Later on, they found they could plant seeds and harvest crops so they began to settle in one place, near a source of water if possible. They built primitive huts for shelter and erected barricades around the huts for protection. They had formed the first tribe. Hence emerged the development of "the herd instinct" where social behaviour and customs became more interdependent.

There must have come a time when these early tribesmen were able to relax, if only for a short time, and contemplate with wonder the world around them. They saw the sun come up each morning and go down at night with a final blaze of colour, and the same old moon which we see today. They saw the beauty of the trees, the sparkling life-saving water, they witnessed the terror of the thunder and lightning.

They saw all this and much more and they must have wondered, how did this happen? How has this dangerous and extraordinary world come about? We still marvel at the wonder of it to this day in our more reflective moments. Our early ancestors thought about it and came up with a conclusion: there must be a greater power up there in the sky, a guiding force on whom we can depend, there must be a God, or even better a group of gods. And this simple belief has been handed down to us. It is ingrained in us from childhood. But today we have more knowledge than our ancestors.

There is no proof or evidence that any kind of god exists. There is only hope which leads to blind faith.

And so, one day in September 1935 at the age of ten I was delivered by my mother to the Royal Masonic Junior School. Soon afterwards, my mother moved to Bristol where she obtained a teaching post and rented the new family home at 4, Henleaze Gardens, Henleaze. My new school was a modern building. It had a Spartan, prison-like look about it but we were greeted with great charm by the senior Master, "Jogger White". However, soon after my mother's tearful departure I was escorted to the charmless F house, one of eight drably identical houses accommodating 50 boys in each house. The House Master was Mr G V Carlin, known as "Givvy". He was a dapper little man and a serious disciplinarian. Every day we were supervised and shepherded from morning to night. We were awakened at 7.30, dressed in silence, proceeded to the Boot Room where we cleaned our boots in silence, then to the Wash Room where we all had our own little basins, washed and cleaned our teeth in silence, then lined up for inspection in silence and marched in crocodiles to the Dining Room and stood in silence at our place at the table until the Duty Master intoned "For what we are about to receive may the Lord make us truly grateful". Then we could talk. If any boy was caught talking during the one hour period from Wake Up Time to Breakfast Time the whole house was punished. If the crime was committed in the Boot Room we all had to go through the boot cleaning ritual about seven or eight times on a Saturday afternoon. If it was committed in the Wash Room then the washing ritual would be carried out, and so on. On certain Saturdays we would have very clean boots or clean teeth, or sometimes even both.

If today you were stranded on a mountain with the darkness and the cold coming down and you had to choose between praying to your god or using your mobile phone, which would you use? Your mobile would bring helicopters, emergency rescuers, what would a god do for you? Nothing. Well, he can't really because he doesn't exist. We go to church and sing "Guide me O thou great redeemer" – why did he guide you to the top of a dangerous mountain in the first place? He's surely falling down on guidance there.

The more we rely on a god to help us, the less we help ourselves. "Ah well," we murmur wisely, "It is God's will, God willing, God help me" and all that nonsense.

I was watching a BBC religious programme recently one Sunday morning. There was a young woman who had made a name for herself as a singer, although I had never heard of her and when she did sing later I was not impressed.

"Yes," says this young woman grandly, "I am certain that my talent is God given, I am blessed in that way so the least I can do is try and develop it to the best of my ability." Heads nod in approval at this wonderful young Christian woman as she casually gives out details of the latest recordings of her God-Given Talent.

Hang on a minute you God-Given Talented lady. Put yourself in the position of a young person in a wheelchair looking at you congratulating yourself on your talent. This person is in a wheelchair because she has a chronic God-given illness or a God-given seriously handicapped body. Or what about the parents of this unfortunate person, who now have to devote their lives and their resources to this unblessed person? If your god is just, why is he so unequal in what he graciously hands out? Have you thought you might just be a little arrogant there? Some of us are dealt pretty awful hands in life, some have better luck. It is just the way things are, so come off it now and show a little modesty.

Of course, if you are a Buddhist you believe that if a person is born disabled, he is being punished for a previous existence. Well, that's alright then, isn't it?

In September 1938 I was moved on to the Senior School which was nearby. This was much better altogether. I loved the buildings and there were extensive playing fields and a beautiful cricket pitch. As a boy in Penarth we had played football, but Givvy Carlin had destroyed a promising soccer career by putting me in goal for some perverse reason. I hated it. Here we played rugby, hockey and cricket. I was put in Latham House with the comparatively amiable "Mug" Tamlyn as my Housemaster. Discipline was reasonably

strict, but fair on the whole. I began to enjoy life again.
I began to do well, in the top three of my class usually,
enjoying sport and making good friends.

On Boxing Day 2004, the world was shocked to learn that there had been a huge underwater explosion in the Indian Ocean area which caused massive tidal waves resulting in a large loss of life. Thousands were suddenly made homeless. This affected people of differing races and religions.

This sort of occurrence is widely known as an Act of God.

Yet people with missing relatives actually prayed to their respective god for their safe delivery - even though they believed the terrible tragedy was caused by this same god. Well, of course he is the Maker of Heaven and Earth, he is the Supreme Being, he knows everything and everybody.

The word god is actually derived from the word good. What was good about the tsunami, as it is now commonly known? Nothing, because it was in fact an Act of Nature with a fairly straightforward explanation. Perhaps it is a consolation to some Christians that the Almighty did actually wait until the day after Christmas Day before wreaking his havoc.

But more of that later, as the Pope said to the Archbishop of Canterbury.

5

Tribal Beginnings

Back to Early Man. As time went on so Man became slightly more sophisticated. They had primitive tools, some better than others. The tools were not only useful but they were no doubt also seen as early "Status Symbols". I wrote earlier that in spite of the wonder and vastness of the universe each person, particularly the male, sees himself as the centre of the universe. Many males strive to be the best, the number one, the alpha male, the natural leader. Those who can't be leader can either strive to topple the leader or wait until a more opportune time comes. We can't all be leaders, anyway.

In every organisation, from the largest to the very smallest, there is a power struggle. We have recently seen this in the Blair/Brown conflict with quite shocking details of rival followers pushing and shoving for supremacy. One of the antagonists may claim to be a devout Christian, and the other may be the son of the manse, but these power struggles are better understood if it is accepted that we all share a common ancestry, that big competitive blob of whatever it is. You will find it in the mightiest boardroom or the tiniest Village Hall committee. The best leaders are the ones who are genuinely accepted by those they lead.

I am not qualified to speak for the female of the species. What mere man is? But in the last fifty years, the often brute physical domination by the male over the female is being replaced by more subtle methods. Many females have found that they have equal or even superior brain power to their male colleagues and are joining the power struggle. Britain has already had its first woman Prime Minister and Hilary Clinton might have become President of the United States. Not long ago a woman's fate was to pursue and win an alpha male to father her children, now they want both family and career and good luck to them.

It is interesting to note that all the religions throughout history have treated women with disdain and even oppression. The Roman Catholic Church does not accept women priests. Only recently the Church of England reluctantly agreed to accept women as clergy, but they are not allowed to be Bishops. In the majority of Mosques women are not even allowed to go through their sacred portals. My advice to any woman in this country who wants to become a priest or a bishop or enter a mosque is to sue the head of the appropriate church. Because sexual discrimination is simply plain illegal under English Law.

But, of course all these out-of-date rules were made several thousand years ago, when women were generally regarded as chattels.

Back to Early Man. As things became easier for those Early Men who had enough food and adequate shelter, they were able to begin to indulge their egotism in other ways. They made tools and pots and other goodies which hopefully other Early Men hadn't got. They became acquisitive.

Imagine a primitive man who is able to provide a choice of caves. A kind of Cave-Agent.

"Good Morning Sir, Good Morning Madam. I'd like to show you this re-furbished cave. Notice the ample supply of running water down the walls. In the outer space here there is an etching of an ape, a very primitive work done by Serious Sid, a very fine Pre-Neanderthal artist. Also we have two benches and a table made from the finest coconut shells. On the left side is the ladies' loo under the bush there, on the right is the men's loo by that tree over there. There's a hole in the roof just here for the barbie. There's a shower over there, only on rainy days I'm afraid. Back there is the bedroom, a little bit dark I'm afraid, but judging by the looks of your missus that's quite a good feature. But it's perfectly dry."

To which his wife, who was a bit of an early Puritan, responds: "If the gods had meant us to keep dry all the time they would have given us umbrellas on the tops of our heads." "Shut up, you silly old fool, we'll take it," says her gallant husband. Already it's all about keeping up with the Joneses.

As the group system developed into the larger tribal element so began the demand for tribal loyalty and this is still deeply implanted in the human psyche. As I have already mentioned, Man was at one time nomadic, but with the advent of farming and growing crops, the ownership of land or territory became important. This led to conflicts between separate groups and has since been the cause of endless wars and disputes between individuals and nation states. "That's mine, that's mine" was and is still the cry today. Over this period too, the tribes invented their own gods to whom they prayed for strength to defeat their enemies. The seeds of different religions were being sown, each one convinced that theirs was the true religion.

Sigmund Freud, who I have already referred to as the accepted founder of psychiatry, also said that civilisation started when one primitive man, instead of throwing back the stone which had been hurled at him, suggested the conflict might be settled by peaceful discussion.

Imagine the scene when King Hugo, an early idealist, stood on a little mound during a pitched battle and said:

"Look here you chaps, why are we throwing these stones at each other? Can't we discuss this matter calmly? (An arrow speeds past him grazing his right arm.)

"Get down, Hugo," said his beautiful queen, Daphne. "These people are Celts, they don't understand reason or anything like that."

"What are Celts, darling?" (Another arrow grazes his left arm.)

"They're awful, darling. Worse than Millwall supporters," cries Daphne in despair.

"No," says Hugo, "I will speak to them." (An arrow pierces his shoulder.) "What are these sticks they are throwing at us?"

"They're called arrows, darling, it's the very latest technology, they are really very dangerous, please do come down," pleaded Daphne.

"No. I must speak to them." (Another arrow pierces his thigh.) "Look, please, we're basically the same people, we've got all we want to eat, we've got our little huts and our land, why can't we meet tomorrow over a cup of coffee and discuss the matter?" (He gasps and fall to the ground as another arrow pierces his heart.)

"Oh, Hugo darling," says Daphne with a tearful sigh, "didn't I warn you they wouldn't listen? At least you tried darling, now you can go before your gods and they will know you have done your best. You're just too good for this world."

Poor Hugo. Alas, the world has seen the loss of many Hugos because Man has followed his basic selfish interests without regard for his fellow creatures. Today, Mankind doesn't need to survive by his more brutish instincts. Be civilised, there's enough for everybody.

In 1939, the war broke out while I was on school holiday in Bristol. We expected all hell to break out with mass bombing of German and British cities. Our elders were distraught, it had only been twenty-one years since the mass slaughter of the 1914-1918 war. So they knew the reality of the situation, we were just mildly excited. When I got back to school I found our dormitories were closed and we had to sleep in bunks under the cloisters. But nothing much happened as the weeks went by. So it was back to the dorms. It was a bit of an anti-climax. But that wasn't to last too long…

6

The Early Civilisations

The early civilisations such as the Egyptian and Babylonian civilisations date back to around 3,500BC. Natural leaders emerged of large groups. They came to be regarded by their followers as not only Kings but as reincarnations of their particular god. The Egyptian civilisation produced the first form of writing, they built beautiful buildings and produced wonderful works of art, as anyone who has visited the Valley of the Nile will testify. Indeed you don't actually have to visit the area as the wonders of modern technology mean you can see them see them on the internet or read about them in the comfort of your own home.

The idea of the leader or King being a reincarnation of their god was a really good wheeze for the Management teams of those days. It was one thing to bring down a tyrannical chief by simply bumping him off. On the other hand it was a very dodgy business to contemplate deposing or even criticising a God-King. Defying mere mortals was one thing, going against a god could risk eternal damnation.

This quite clever practise did have the advantage of giving stability to a tribe or country, which enabled Science and Discovery to be pursued. It was also, however, despotic and hierarchical, which resulted in a very uneven distribution of income, to say the least. It also resulted in the introduction of a class system, where the top echelon of people became educated and the vast majority of people remained uninformed and had to live off "pickings from the rich man's table".

This is amply illustrated by the recent exhibition in London where the opulent treasures of King Tutankhamen were exhibited. The mistaken belief about their unverified gods was that they would be pleased to receive large quantities of earthly goods from their departed kings and leading citizens. It was thought that this might help them on the way to a permanent life in Paradise. But the gods were pretty remiss in not claiming their treasures.

The treasure which has been found in the young King's tomb is truly amazing. It illustrates the degree of brilliant design and craftsmanship which was evident at that time. It also illustrates the error of inventing all-powerful spurious gods, usually embroidered in a mass of detail without any evidence of their existence. Similar tombs placed around ancient Egypt were robbed. King Tut's was well concealed and spared for many years until discovered by an Englishman in 1922. Naturally, the legend spread that the gods had put a curse on anyone who entered his tomb. Well, that's another good wheeze to deter robbers, isn't it?

The belief of the Divine Right of Kings persisted for several centuries, and has been a useful tool in keeping the masses in order in many countries. Henry VIII used it to break away from the Roman Catholic Church. Consult your History teacher to find out when it was abandoned. I can, however, tell you with absolute authority that the concept of God-Emperor was only abandoned by the Japanese after the Second World War, after some slight persuasion by the USA.

But, in spite of their faults, the Egyptian civilisation added knowledge to the benefit of future generations. There were also useful contributions to the civilisation process by the Babylonians, the Minoan era in Crete, who first introduced pen and ink writing, and from other areas in the Middle East and southern Europe. On the other side of the world, China too had its golden age of discovery. All of these countries had their own particular gods, and all were convinced that theirs were the only true god.

With the exception of China, which is now emerging as a huge economic power, it is interesting to note that the areas where the civilisation processes first thrived are now generally lagging behind. But China is still best known today for its repressive government, general poverty, cheap goods and its worldwide take-aways with its portions of Number Eight or whatever number took your fancy. As for the Middle East, most of its energies are squandered into squabbling about religions. Only the huge natural oil sources with which Nature has bestowed them has saved them from abject poverty.

In May 1940, events began to unfold, both on a national and personal scale.

After completing their conquest of Norway, the Germans launched a huge offensive on the Western Front. By-passing the so-called impregnable Maginot Line, the Germans went through the Netherlands at break-neck speed and were in Paris in just over three weeks. The British were forced to make a humiliating retreat from Dunkirk.

One morning in late May I was awakened at 5am by one of the masters who told me my mother was seriously ill and I had to go to Bristol that morning. I arrived to find my mother in a coma. I was told she was suffering from kidney failure. Two days later, she died.

The most interesting early civilisation was that of the Greeks. They were the first to challenge the authority of the early God-Kings. There was a man called Democritus. He discussed the possibility that a State, as a comparatively smaller collection of people sharing the same language came to be known, might actually be governed by consent of the members of that state.

In 500 BC the first democratic state of Athens was proclaimed. Freedom of choice did not apply to Athenian slaves, who were simply recognised only as some citizen's rightful property. In this respect they acted in a similar fashion to the instigators of the American constitution which was introduced in 1789 AD, over two thousand years later. Slow progress there, I fear.

The Greeks were thinkers. They spent most of their time thinking and then tried to put the results of their thinking into action. They produced great sculptures, buildings, open-air theatres. They also produced scientists, philosophers, mathematicians, artists, and playwrights. One of their greatest philosophers was Aristotle, who, unhampered by the idea of divine influences, thought that logic was the first step towards scientific knowledge. He also believed that happiness was not brought by wealth, pleasure or fame but by the pursuit of truth. There's a refreshing thought for the "celebrity" obsessed thousands who sit goggled-eyed at the television every night.

Socrates was possibly the greatest of all the Ancient Greeks. He lived for 91 years. He was a teacher of wisdom:

he believed that virtue is knowledge, that all wickedness is caused by ignorance. He made biting criticisms of any practises he considered wrong. He was tried, convicted and sentenced to death for corrupting young people. He was merely telling the truth as he saw it. He cheated his executioners by taking hemlock. Ancient Greece wasn't all plain sailing.

Ordinary people are scared sometimes of new thinking. It makes them feel inferior. It's just a chip off the old blob.

Plato was a pupil of Socrates and was greatly influenced by him. He also felt deeply about the lowly status of women in Greek Society. He claimed that women were not just "busts and bottoms", to put the current phrase more politely, and argued it was possible to have a "platonic" relationship with a woman without sex being involved. This was an enormous step forward which has still not been universally accepted.

Archimedes was a mathematician, astronomer, inventor, a brilliant man. He was famous for shouting out "Eureka" when stepping into his bath and causing it to overflow, and running down the street shouting joyfully that he had confirmed his theory of water displacement. Yes, well, the first part of the sentence is probably true.

He is also credited with inventing the screw and the wheel. The latter was a huge step forward in the moving of heavy objects. You can imagine the pampered classes whingeing: "What do we want wheels for? The slaves are idle enough already…"

Pythagorus was also a mathematician. We are all familiar with his famous theorem, where he showed that the squares… er… that is the sum of the squares on a right angled rectangle... or was it a triangle... was equal to the... what was it called... the hotpotenuse... Well we all know it, don't we, that goes without saying, we all think about it every day.

Then there were the playwrights, Aristophanes, the satirist whose plays can probably be more readily appreciated by modern audiences than the other great writers such as Aeschyllus, Euripides and Sophocles whose plays were on a grander scale and can be a bit heavy going without some pre-study. These writers were the pioneers of theatre and their influence is still evident today.

The Greek gods were departmentalised, as it were. Eros was the god of love, Apollo the god of beauty, Nike the god of victory and there were many many more. Zeus was a very big wheel, he was the King of Gods. They are, however, described as mythical gods. The playwrights and story tellers weaved their writings around these gods who got up to the most fantastic things like piercing young lovers with arrows and turning the object of their affection into donkeys and various other skylarks. The stories were in fact drawing parables and making points of view from their mythical behaviour. But it was all mythology.

My suspicion is that the Greeks did not believe in any gods at all. Their discoveries and philosophies were all derived from rational and logical thinking. Therein lies the cause of their true greatness.

It is impossible to do justice to the contribution that the Ancient Greeks made to the sum of human knowledge in a couple of paragraphs. If you are bored with life, dear teenager, why not study them in closer detail. Don't forget either that they were the founders of the Olympic games and modern sport.

But how can we possibly be good boys and girls without a God to punish us or reward us? Why should only the religious, the unthinking faithful, hold the High Moral Ground? How does the poor developing, improving, irreligious human animal reach the High Moral Ground? Read on, read on. All will be revealed, as the window cleaner said when he was cleaning the bathroom windows.

So, a couple of weeks after my fifteenth birthday, I found myself an orphan. After my father died, my mother and I had become close. She was a very beautiful, intelligent woman but always liable to mood swings. She had a wonderfully hearty, infectious laugh which could be followed quite quickly by sudden rages. She worried a lot and because we boys were at boarding school she was lonely most of the time. I think she alienated my elder brothers with her emotional outbursts. They both grew up to be very British: too much emotion wasn't on the menu. Although I was the youngest, I somehow felt responsible for her wellbeing and happiness. In her calmer moments she was a great support for me and always encouraged me. She was only forty-eight when she died. It is a terrible thing to say perhaps, but in a sense I was relieved that I no longer had responsibility on my young shoulders for her happiness. She had been my guiding light: whatever I did, I always considered if my mother would approve or not. That didn't always stop me doing it, but that was the way my mind worked. And continued to do so for many years.

7

How to reach the Moral High Ground

If you read the Old Testament, which is pretty gory and in my view not at all suitable for children, or indeed for adults for that matter, you will learn how Moses claimed the Moral High Ground. When I was fifteen I had to study the Book of Kings in the Old Testament for a subject we called "Scripture" in those days.

I couldn't read it with any enthusiasm as it struck me as being very violent. There was a lot of talk about people sticking swords in their enemies' groins, bowels gushing out and horses' hamstrings being cut. And this is the Good Book. Eventually I refused to read it.

When I came to take my School Certificate examination (the equivalent of "O" levels or GCSEs) I nervously and furtively wrote on the exam paper that I could not answer any of the questions because I found that what little I had read of the book of Kings utterly repugnant. I expected to be whipped, thrown out of school, perhaps even put in gaol for Blasphemy, which is still a crime in British Law to this very day by the way. None of this happened, I am glad to say, although the results recorded, not unsurprisingly, that I had failed in Scripture.

But in order to research this book I had to research parts of the Bible again and I found the story of Moses leading his people to the "Promised Land" equally repugnant.

In those days God used to "spake" unto the various prophets and they used to spake back to him on a regular basis, being told what to do.

This practise seems to have stopped in modern times.

I would spend the school holidays at the homes of various boys from school. The first time was with an older boy who lived at a little village between Weston-super-Mare and Bristol. It was a disaster, we had very little in common. His mother had married again to what they used to call "a gentleman farmer" and they ran a small farm. One day they entertained a retired colonel and his very grand wife to tea, a very intimidating lady. They had a daughter, a girl of about sixteen. The colonel, who was quite a jolly chap, suggested she and I went for a walk. So... we went for a walk... just imagine... me with a girl... I had hardly spoken with a girl before... I don't think I'd ever been alone with one before. I can't remember the conversation but it must have been stilted. But Rose was confident and she took complete charge. We came to a sheltered spot. Let's sit down, she said. Within seconds we were groping each other and kissing. After about ten minutes of this she said briskly: "Come on, we'd better get back." I had the feeling I had failed some kind of test.

Other holidays were more successful, one with a friend in Sunderland, another in Sheffield. Eventually my father's sister Joan heard of my plight and she more or less agreed to take me over, although we had only briefly met when I was a little boy. She lived in Liverpool. Just before Christmas 1940 I arrived at Lime Street Station and was met by my Aunt Joan, a small, stout, florid Scottish lady. She took me to her tiny council house in Clubmoor, one of the grottier suburbs of Liverpool. We had hardly finished a wartime meal when the sirens went and we retreated to the Anderson shelter in the tiny back garden. The raids were severe, not so severe as the subsequent May blitz of 1941 but bad enough. We learned later that an ammunition train had been hit in a siding nearby and this went off at regular intervals. The raids went on for three nights, but stopped for the Christmas period. My poor aunt was terrified. Her husband Uncle Bill was a really kind man. He was a dock labourer, my aunt's second husband. Her first husband had been a prosperous coal merchant in Glasgow but he was killed in an accident, so poor Aunt Joan was forced to marry "beneath her". They were very hard up. In those days the docks used to operate a "pen" system. The dockers would stand in this cattle-like pen and the foremen would choose as many men as they needed - the rest were sent home. They also spent a lot of time on strike, trying to get a minimum guaranteed wage. I was seeing the other side of the coin. That is why I became a "lefty" - but not for long.

I'd like to put to you a lighter version of the description of the biblical version of Moses leading the Israelites out of Egypt to the Promised Land. The language and the style may be different but the following story contains the essential ingredients of what is written in the Book of Genesis. Having seen the Hollywood blockbuster years ago in which Charlton Heston played Moses with his homely American accent, I have to admit that has been an influence.

"Oh, Hi God, yeah, this is Moses…

Well of course I'd like to take my people back to Israel, I'm sick to death being bossed about by these Egyptians, only last week they got us trying to make bricks out of straw, not easy I can tell you…

Go tell Pharaoh we want to go home? Well, I'm just an old man, he ain't going to listen to me...

I'm your representative on earth? Gee, thanks God, I sure do appreciate that...

Have I got a rod or a staff? Aaron, have we got a rod or a staff? We got a walking stick, is that OK?...

OK, so we tell Aaron to go see Pharaoh, strike the walking stick three times in front of him... then it will turn into a serpent? You don't say! Oh, he's dead scared of serpents, he's a real cissy...

Is that right? That'll convince Fairyboy he's working for you... then Aaron tells him we're all going home... and if he don't like that you will turn all the rivers and the water into blood... say, that is one great idea!...

Say, can we have a dummy run on this serpent thing? So, here goes, three knocks on the floor with the stick... oh my god! We sure have got a serpent! Yeah, yeah, OK, down boy, now keep calm, no need to wrap yourself around me... Say, how do we get rid of it, God? Just knock four times with the stick? OK... gee, that's better... that sure is some serpent..."

So, Aaron goes round to see Fairyboy, knocks three times with the stick and up comes the serpent, so Fairyboy brings on about twenty of his own serpents and our serpent immediately gobbles them all up. And then Aaron tells him "if our people can't go home God will turn all the rivers into blood".

So Fairyboy says "I suppose you think you're clever because your serpents ate all my serpents... and as for you lot" (he turns to his magicians) "call yourself magicians, if you can't do better than this you'll find yourself on pyramid building double quick, and you won't like that, will you… and as for you, Mr Airbrush or whatever your name is, you can go back to your little god and tell him you can't frighten Pharaoh. We've got our own gods. Pharaoh can fix you and your brother Moses. Pharaoh tough hombre. You lot will stay here as long as I say, you Israelites are all stinkers but we need you to build our new sewage system."

So God turned all the rivers into blood. Fairyboy wasn't as tough as he thought. He sent for Aaron right away, he was doing his nut. "We've got no water," he says hysterically, "all the fish are dying, the cattle are dying, I haven't had a drink for days, I'm so thirsty. Alright then, get your people out of Egypt and good riddance to you."

So God turned all the waters back into water, but soon after this Pharaoh went back on his word. In fact he did this four more times, so God caused a plague of flies, then frogs, then he brought the cattle out in blisters (would that be the dreaded foot and mouth?) and then locusts. Each time Pharaoh promised to comply and each time he went back on his promise.

So God spake unto Moses again.

"Yeah, I totally agree, something really drastic is needed…

What's that? Kill the first born male child in every family?…

Yeah, well, that sure is drastic, you can't argue with that… but what about our first born, are they going to be OK?

You've thought of that… yeah, yeah, I'm listening… Each family kill a lamb and smear the blood over the front door... right... and then we hang a thyssom plant over our front door... what exactly is a thyssom plant? ... OK, don't get angry, yeah, we'll go ask at a garden centre... this way you will pass over every Israelite house... and every one of our children will be spared... my god that is neat, that is really neat...

Henceforth this day can be celebrated as the Feast of the Passover... oh my God, that is really clever, but don't you think that's a little vindictive to the Ay-rabs... that's just too bad? OK, I'll get on to that right away."

And so it came to pass and Fairyboy was very angry, to put it mildly, and he said "I'll get even with you even if it takes two thousand years"... and they're still trying.

So Moses says "Abe, Solly, Hymie, Ikey, come on, get the rest of the lads, get the families moving and the cattle, we are going to the Promised Land".

A few days later they hit the Red Sea. So Moses spake unto God again.

"Hi, there God, its Mo again...

Yeah, everything is pretty good... we've just got a couple of problems... we'd like your help in getting across the Red Sea...

What's that? You'll arrange for the parting of the waves at 1500 hours? That's great...

If I can get them all across in two hours you'll be able to drown the Ay-rabs who'll be chasing after us when you close the waves... oh, that's really great...

The other thing is, we've got no food...

Oh, you'll send down some manna from heaven right away? Say, what exactly is manna?... I see... it's wheatmeal, very nutritious... I see...

Any chance of some hamburgers and French fries for the kids? I see, don't push it... OK. Thanks a lot, we'll be ready at three o'clock."

The kids didn't think much of the manna, but that's kids today, they get everything they want, you just can't please them. Just wait till they see the parting of the waves. Disneyland will have nothing on this.

"OK everybody. Three o'clock. I can hear the water parting...

Just look at this! Boy, this is going to make a great movie! OK you guys, let's go!

THE HEBREWS ARE COMING... Everybody sing:

Over there, over there, have no fears, shed no tears over there

'Cos the Brews are coming, the Brews are coming

And we ain't coming back 'cos we're staying over here..."

And they were over in the scheduled two hours.

Then Aaron began to get very excited.

"Will you take a look at that! Look at those guys coming after us... and the water is closing... wahey! All the riders thrown off their horses into the sea! Look at them just gurgling away... this is great stuff!"

"Calm down," says Moses to Aaron, "we've got a new religion starting here, we've got to claim the Moral High Ground... what for? We've got to show them we're nice people, that we love everybody... yeah, especially the Ay-rabs. I'll get on to God again, what we need is a set of guidelines, a set of rules."

"Hi god, it's Mo again…

Oh you saw it all, did you? You've done a great job there… sure it was great to see them all drowning…

But look, I don't want to be disrespectful… but don't you think it was just a little teeny bit vindictive?… Sure, I know, they treated us badly… but there is such a thing as forgiveness…

An eye for an eye and a tooth for a tooth?… Yeah, fine, but we sure could have a lot of one-eyed gummies walking about… what about turning the other cheek? Oh great, you'll give it some thought…

You'll send us some tablets? Oh, thank you God.

Well whaddya know, here they are, these two little capsules… Let's take a look. To be taken twice daily. Don't kill, don't screw around, especially if you're married, don't steal your neighbour's ox or his i-pod… love your neighbour as yourself, that could be a tough one. Don't tell fibs, look after your old folks, yeah that's all good stuff, but here's the big one… thou shalt have no other gods but me, me, me, just remember, I'm the boss… yeah, OK, but that could be a problem…anyway, I'll read them all later."

And that is how the Jewish religion was started.

And that is why the State of Israel was proclaimed in 1948 for the Jewish people because it was their Promised Land.

It must be true 'cos I read it in the Bible, didn't you?

In July 1941 I had reached the age of 16. I had just taken my School Certificate. I later learned I had passed with five credits and three passes, one failure in

Scripture, I may have mentioned that already. Not bad, but not brilliant. In those days higher education was only for those who hoped to go to University. Eighteen months earlier I had been one of the bright lights of my year, but more recently I had dropped to the lower end of the class. It would be easy to blame my mother's death for this, but that would have been unfair. There was just a kind of malaise enveloping me, probably something to do with my hormones. I entered a dream-like world of my own. I was not invited to stay on for the Sixth Form.

During my school days my great ambition had been to get into the School Play, but at the audition I would stammer and go red and make a terrible botch of it. However, I did make a modest hit when I spoke in a Desert Island debate. We were invited to take the part of a well-known person stranded on a desert island. Food was short and each person had to convince the audience that he should not be eaten. I chose to impersonate a little known music hall artist who had taken my fancy. His name was Oliver Wakefield and he was billed as the Voice of Inexperience, a sort of typical English twit. My opening lines were: "It gives me great pleasure to be able to undress... sorry... address... such a large body." Everybody laughed. I was encouraged. I continued, they carried on laughing. From then on I was hooked. I just wanted to be an actor.

8

The Romans and the life of Jesus

Then, of course, there was the Roman Civilisation. They shared their gods with the Greeks but they gave them different names, just to confuse everybody. For instance the god of love became Cupid instead of Eros, the god of beauty Venus instead of Apollo. Like the Greeks, again, they were mainly mythical and didn't really bother with gods which allowed them to get on with what they did best.

And what they did best was conquering most of the Western and Mediterranean world, making straight roads, having orgies, pioneering sanitation, Roman baths, staging sadistic gladiatorial contests, good engineering and ruthless in-fighting for the top positions. It lasted 400 years. Before it collapsed it converted to Christianity. Verdict: Good practical progress, bit of a nasty lot though.

It is interesting to remind ourselves that most words in the English language have their root in either Latin or Ancient Greek. I opened an English dictionary at random. I found the word lobby, from the Latin *lobia*, a porch. I then looked at lobe (of the ear) from the Greek *lobos*, meaning the lobe of the ear. So we have to thank them for our glorious English language, which I hope I am not mutilating too much.

During the time of the Roman Empire, there came to the Holy Land a man called Jesus. The term Holy Land is surely the greatest misnomer of all time as it must be the unholiest land in the world. It is full of people who have made a profession of squabbling about their various gods.

Anyone who thought that Tony Blair invented "spin" must goggle with wonder at the spin around Jesus Christ. What a CV he was given!

- He could walk on water.

- He could bring the dead back to life.

- He could cure any disease with a wave of his hand.

- He could clone dead fishes, probably could do the same with meat pies.

- He could produce hundreds of loaves at will. Sliced or wholemeal.

- His mother was a virgin and he was the son of God.

- And if you believed in him you would live forever in Heaven, every mod con.

- And if you didn't you would burn in Hell.

- And by the way, there's only one true god. My dad.

- All the others are ditched.

Well, there's no argument, is there. Go for it.

I'm sure that Jesus was really a very nice chap. He probably did think he was the son of god, but he must have known all the other stuff about walking on water and the loaves and fishes was invented by his followers. If he was alive today he'd probably be a Liberal Democrat, he had the sandals and he was a little bit woolly. All that stuff about miracles was probably dreamed up by the local hacks, just as they built up Wayne Rooney who was going to win the World Cup for England.

What he was saying was really just be nice to each other. He also probably believed in Heaven and Hell, so did millions of people who came before and after him. But where is the evidence for that belief? A few contradictory statements from the remote past in the shape of ancient books is not enough.

On leaving school in 1941 I had no means of support. My mother had left me £200 in trust until I was twenty-one. I had two joint legal guardians, one was a Mr Biggs. He had a son called Robert who was a close friend of my brother Jim, so Jim was looked after for a while by the Biggs family. My eldest brother, Ian, was in the Army. My other guardian was the Headmaster of Colston's School. How that came about I shall never know, but I never had the privilege of meeting him. So I was obliged to impose myself on my aunt in Liverpool. She was a very well-meaning lady, a Scottish Presbyterian. I decided to go off for a while.

I borrowed a bicycle from a kindly neighbour and went off to see, firstly, my school friend in Sheffield, and then on to my friend in Sunderland. On the way back I called on my mother's brother who lived near Durham. I can't remember if my Uncle Walter and his wife were pleased to meet me, but they can't have openly objected as I stayed with them without invitation for about two weeks. Looking back on that trip, I have no memory of how it was funded. I simply imposed myself on people and accepted their hospitality without even thinking that I might be a burden. Such is the complete selfishness of the teenager. I suppose people were sorry for me because I had been orphaned, but I never consciously exploited that situation, I just took it all for granted. I must have been away for at least six weeks. When I got back to Liverpool, the neighbour was none too pleased about being without his bike for such a long while.

My aunt, who was not well off, firmly suggested I should think about getting a job. I felt very guilty because the work ethic had been firmly implanted in me by my mother and the masters at my school. I knew very little of the outside world. I wanted to do something exciting, but I had no idea how to go about it. My aunt suggested I get a job with the Liverpool Corporation, there was a pension scheme. Well, that was of vital importance at my age, wasn't it? I started work in the City Treasurer's Department in Dale Street. It wasn't the least bit exciting.

Because of our herd instincts inherited from our blobby ancestors, anyone who doesn't conform is liable to suspicion. So the local Scribes and Pharisees who controlled the local population became displeased at Jesus. This young upstart was usurping their little domain, so they complained to the Roman Governor, Pontius Pilate.

There are four different written versions of what happened next. But the consensus seems to have been that Jesus claimed to be King of the Jews and the Son of God, which got up the noses of the local big-wigs. This privately must have amused Pilate as he well knew he had battalions of thuggish Roman soldiers who kept the Jewish people under heel. So Pilate famously replied that "he saw no harm in this man".

Well, he certainly wasn't a threat to the Romans. Pilate knew that the callous, brutal bunch of blobs back in Rome HQ would have a good laugh at anyone who said "blessed are the meek".

The feast of the Passover was coming up. As a token gesture, the kindly Roman chief gangsters allowed their local Governors to reprieve one Jewish offender in deference to the Jewish feast. Pilate offered them either Barrabas, a small time crook, or Jesus for reprieve. But the crowd bayed and clamoured for the death of Jesus.

And so he was taken out and nailed to two pieces of wood where he endured a slow and agonising death before a huge mocking, jeering crowd, like a football crowd, all mouthing witty things such as "if you all hate Jesus clap your hands…"

And so the little blob of whatever struck again. The all-consuming drive for survival won the day. Pilate took the line of least resistance. The Jewish crowd were satisfied that their comfortable beliefs were protected. And they had a great day out.

Jesus Christ was probably the first man in recorded history to see existence not just as a struggle for individual or factional survival but simply as a person who tried to spread gentleness, understanding and goodwill to all his fellow creatures. The ethics and standards of Christianity are mainly good, as they are in many religions. The belief in an afterlife with its rewards for "good behaviour" is in my view mistaken. Virtue has its own rewards.

But what is claimed to have happened afterwards is even more extraordinary.

As before, accounts vary, but it appears that his body was placed in a tomb. After about three days he is said to have risen from the dead, left the tomb, called on Mary Magdalene for a goodbye kiss, had a chat with his disciples while frightening the life out of some people on the way. However, after assuring everyone he was OK, he is said to have ascended into Heaven where he sits on the right hand of God. He also promised he would return to Earth one day.

There are grown up, otherwise intelligent, educated people who actually believe this. In fact, some people thought he'd come back as Tony Blair, but that didn't last too long.

And that's why we have chocolate eggs for Easter and Santa Claus comes round every Christmas with presents for the kiddy-winks, which is good news for the retail trade.

The office in Liverpool was almost Dickensian. High stools and large leather-bound ledgers. The office was full of detached middle-aged men condemned to a life of entering figures in dusty books. The office was open to the public; there was a small window and a bell. As the Junior member of staff I was delegated to answer the bell. I was greeted by irate rate-payers. I soon discovered that all rate-payers were irate. They would shove a piece of paper under my nose demanding to know "the meaning of this". "This" was usually a letter from the City Treasurer demanding something or other, usually money. I would go round the middle-aged gentlemen, pleading for information. They each in turn referred me to other middle-aged gentlemen, all in vain. I quickly developed a technique of confidently saying, "Ah, you need the office along the corridor". Nobody ever came back.

I was completely broke. My monthly salary was £3, nearly all of which went to my aunt, my uncle now being in bad health. I spent my lunch hour looking for more interesting work. A favourite was to go to the Liverpool Playhouse in Williamson Square and knock on the stage door in the hope of getting a job. I would stand for half an hour trying to pluck up enough courage to go in and ask. But I never did - after all, what did I know about the theatre? Then I would slink back to the office, defeated. I went to shipping offices to see if I could get away to sea, but I was always referred somewhere else. At 5pm I would join the queue at the back of St George's Hall, usually in the pouring rain, to fight my way on to an overcrowded number 13 or 14 tram. I remember spending my 17th birthday going for a solitary walk feeling distinctly suicidal. I joined the Home Guard, that was better.

I volunteered to join the Navy as a Fleet Air Arm pilot. At the end of my medical a gorgeous but very superior Wren displayed a large open book showing a mass of colours. In a bored voice she told me there was a large figure showing on the page, could I tell her what it was. Is that a little three in the corner there, I suggested tentatively. She gave me a withering look, and showed me further pages without success. I was ushered before the doctor. In a hushed tone he told me I'd got DCV. I went pale, immediately visualising the next three years in an iron lung. Yes, he continued, you couldn't possibly become a pilot with defective colour vision.

I had decided to apply for the Navy as you could be accepted if you were under eighteen. Apart from my DCV I had been pronounced fit, so in February 1943 I reported for my initial training at HMS Royal Arthur, Skegness. This turned out to be Billy Butlin's holiday camp. The Shakespearian quote above the main gate, "Our true intent is all for your delight" was not really appropriate.

Incidentally, DCV is not to be confused with colour blindness, that is a very rare condition, it is a failure to distinguish varying shades of colour. That is why I like bold colours. By the way, until I joined the Navy, we were losing.

9

The rites and wrongs of religions

So, all over the world there are these strange instructions going out from the various religious big wigs. Such as:

- Don't work on the Sabbath, which is Sunday, except when it's Saturday.

- And don't eat pork or bacon. Or no meat at all unless it's kosher, where the animal has to be killed in a particularly nasty way.

- Eat only fish on a Friday.

- Go to communion on a Sunday and partake of the blood and flesh of Jesus (which strikes me as being slightly cannibalistic).

- Do not forget the cow is a holy animal and may defecate anywhere it wishes.

- And if you're born a Jew, off comes your foreskin... ouch. Which, in some mysterious way, is supposed to cleanse you spiritually.

- Or if you're a young African woman you can have your clitoris cut off, which stops you enjoying sex, so you can concentrate on doing the washing if you are fortunate enough to find any water.

- No French letters for you, me boyo, and if you're a priest, no nookie.

- Or never cut your hair or beard and cover your head with a turban.

- Or wrap some bombs around your waist and blow up anyone you don't like.

- Or, if you're a woman, cover your head in church, perhaps even in public. Or better still, don't even come to church, remember you're only a woman.

- Or, if you're seriously mentally or physically handicapped, it's because you were a bad boy in a previous life, even though you can't remember it.

- Failure to carry out these instructions is a sin.

- Which, in some religions, can fortunately be forgiven.

- But in other religions can result in getting stoned.

- But not the way you get stoned on a Saturday night.

- And also sometimes on a Friday night for good measure.

And many, many more. Rules and regulations, that is.

Then, of course all these religions have their differences.

These are called Schisms.

The schisms of the isms is the very depth of disputisms.

In the early 16th Century, Henry VIII ascended the throne of England. He was a competent, handsome young man, a squashbuckling, hard drinking, eye-wandering lech, the James Bond of his day. He married Catharine of Aragon, a Spanish, Roman Catholic princess. She gave birth to a daughter, Mary. But by 1534 Henry had become fat, bloated, ugly and discontented because she had failed to produce a male heir. But he still had his wandering eye and he fancied the young Ann Boleyn who he thought might also bring him a male heir.

This happy thought was fraught with difficulties because Cath was a Catholic and the big boss Pope in Rome did not countenance divorce. To marry Ann would mean ex-communication from the Church of Rome and eternal damnation. So Henry was swayed by his good old blob ancestry and pursued his blob-given urge to propagate the species. And there was good sport in the making, as Master Will Shakespeare so succinctly put it. But alas she only managed to give him a daughter (who just happened to turn out to be one of the greatest sovereigns we ever had). So Henry gallantly had Ann beheaded on some trumped-up charge.

Henry had reasoned, "I'm King by Divine Right, aren't I? So I can do what I want, can't I? I'll make my own Archbishops and Bishops, and while I'm about it, we'll get rid of all those monks moaning away in their monasteries, there must be a fair bit of loot there for the taking, so send that Ann Boleyn a bunch of flowers and tell her to pop round tonight."

This was nothing to do with faith, belief, theology or conviction. The Protestant Church of England was formed simply so that Henry could secure a divorce and marry a woman with better child-bearing prospects.

As a result there were years of bloody conflict between Catholics and Protestants which continues to this very day.

And then, the newly founded C of E started schisming. There were Baptists, Methodists, Presbyterians, Congregationalists, Unitarians, Sixth Day Adventists, or was it Fifth Day Adventists, lots more anyway.

Now, of course the Church of England faces another big schism over the Homosexuality Issue. Homosexuality was declared legal in Britain over forty years ago. But large sections of the C of E do not wish to recognise this and are refusing to allow homosexuals to be made bishops.

I trained as a Wireless Operator in Earl's Court. The course lasted four months. We were in civilian billets, five to a room in a small crowded hotel. The food was terrible, even allowing for wartime difficulties. We spent the days labouring with the dots and the dashes of the Morse code, now alas completely redundant. We spent the evenings discovering the delights of our Capital city. To this very day, whenever I travel on the underground, I automatically start transposing the adverts opposite my seat into Morse code. I can still read Morse code at the required 20 words per minute. In late 1943 I joined the ship's company of HMS Ambuscade which was tied up alongside Gourock pier on the Clyde. The advantage of being on the Ambuscade was, as it was a very old ship, it kept breaking down, so we spent a lot of time in the Glasgow dockyards undergoing boiler cleans, refits or repairs. In the evenings we would patrol the Glasgow pubs for beer which tended to run out of supplies about 9pm. When she was sea worthy, we could steam along at 32 knots which was really exhilarating.

We were based at the lovely harbour of Campbeltown in Argyllshire, developing anti-submarine detection equipment (asdic). One of our submarines would go out to sea and we would try to detect it. As Germany began to lose the war, in desperation her U-boats were ordered to increase their efforts against our shipping and would come ever closer to our shores. As we had the most up to date asdic equipment, we were frequently ordered to get out to 12 West and start sweeping for U-boats. I found that a sea-going life is only interesting when you get ashore. It can be tedious. We "sparkers" and our Coders had to operate a four-on, four-off watch system. For four hours we would take down broadcast messages in code. When we were relieved we crept into our hammocks with Morse code signals still pouring into our addled brains. Cooked food was mostly not possible because of a pitching, rolling galley, so we existed mainly on corned beef sandwiches and "kye", a thick chocolate drink concoction. We spent long periods not knowing what day or what time it was, tossing about in the Atlantic, just off the west coast of Ireland. When we got a contact on the asdic, the echoing "ping" was put on broadcast through the ship. Action stations were called and the ping would get louder as the contact became nearer. Then we would drop depth charges or fire our Squid at the unfortunate chaps below. This was always in company with other ships so we never knew at our level if we had been successful or not. This went on for months as we met convoys who had just crossed the pond and escorted them to safe waters.

One incident I can recall in detail. Thanks to the wonders of the internet I can tell you that on September 1st 1944, HMS Hurst Castle, a newly commissioned Castle Class Corvette, was torpedoed and sunk by U-482 at 0822 hours at 12 West, north of Troy Island. The entire crew of 105 was recovered and taken on board by HMS Ambuscade. I can vouch for that because I had just come off the Morning Watch (4am-8am). I had gone out on the main deck for a stretch and a breath of fresh air. We were cruising along, six ships in line abreast, at one end of the line was Hurst

Castle, about half a mile away on our starboard beam. There was an explosion, and quite suddenly I could see lots of figures appearing on the deck. After only two minutes her stern went up and she disappeared into the deep. We steamed gently up to the survivors and got the scrambling nets over the side. We pulled them aboard, covered in oil, shocked but relieved. It was a miracle they all survived, their ship had gone down so quickly. They stripped naked and we hosed them down, covered them in blankets, the coxswain got the rum out and we put them ashore at Londonderry. The ship was filthy, it took several days to get rid of all the oil. The European war ended in May 1945. We braced ourselves for service in the Far East but then came the Atomic Bomb and it was all over.

So why can't we accept homosexuals? That's right, it's in the Bible. So it's got to be right, hasn't it? So where actually is it written in the Bible? In the Book of Leviticus, Chapter 20, Verse 13. I quote from the Knox version of the Bible (School edition, and recognised by the hierarchy of the Church of England, Scotland and Wales):

"No mercy, either when a man has commerce with another man as if he had been a woman; either is guilty of a foul deed and both must die."

So who wrote this book of Leviticus? Apparently it's written by a chap called Levi, the third son of Jacob, and is largely an alleged summary of an imaginary god's conversations with Moses. It is also a manual for priests on how to make burnt or unburnt sacrifices. I invite readers to take out their bible (or borrow one) and have a little browse through this vindictive rambling. Let me give you a few samples.

"If a man has commerce [that doesn't mean selling them lollipops or ice creams, it means having sex] with a slave woman promised in marriage, but not yet redeemed or set free, both shall be beaten, but they shall not be put to death as if she were a free woman. The man must offer a ram to the Lord at the tabernacle door for wrong done, and so the priest will make intercession before the fault has committed, and the Lord will be merciful, and pardon his fault."

So if you're going to have illicit sex, make sure it's with a slave, you'll only be beaten.

There are twenty-seven chapters telling you what you must not do, most of which you don't really want to do anyway, and graphic descriptions of the way blood sacrifices must be made. Such as:

"And this is the rule which governs the offering of a victim for wrong done, its blood must be poured around the altar, the parts which are offered must be the tail, and the fat which covers the entrails, the two kidneys and the fat which is close to them, and with the kidneys the caul of the liver. All these the priest will burn on the altar as a burnt sacrifice to the Lord for the wrong doing, the flesh of the victim is set apart for holy uses, but it may be used for any male member of the priestly family."

Nothing for the missus then.

If a wrong doer cannot afford to offer a lamb or a goat for sacrifice, the priest will accept two turtle doves or two young pigeons, but this must be accompanied by a quantity of flour.

More serious transgressors may be stoned or burned to death. As for women who menstruate, "they must remain apart because of their monthly time, women who have a continuance issue of blood, and men with whom such women have commerce". Women were generally regarded as unclean.

These are ramblings of an ancient "prophet" setting down a description of conversations between an unknown god and Moses which allegedly took place about 3000 years ago. These ramblings originate from various Greek and Hebrew ancient books and were then translated into Latin in the 4th Century AD by a chap called Jerome, and eventually translated into English in the 17th Century and published as the Authorised Version in the reign of King James the First.

There still remains a revulsion against homosexual practise by a large proportion of the world's population, but it is now on the way to being universally accepted by fair-minded thinking people. Homosexuals have made huge contributions to the civilisation process. In Darwinian terms it can perhaps be caused by a little twitch in the blob. In any case, one is born that way, just as one may be born with red hair or blue or brown eyes, and there is nothing that can be done about it. Most homosexuals are happy as they are and they do no harm to other people. So let them be and judge them on their merits or de-merits as you would any other people.

The idea of these robed and mitred gentlemen (and unmitred ladies) solemnly discussing whether a homosexual gentleman may or may not become a bishop of their esteemed establishment on the basis of the repugnant writings and ancient, remote diktats of Mr Levi is preposterous. Why don't they just admit they don't like gays? In any case, as I have already said, what the Church of England is attempting to do is against the British laws of discrimination.

When lovely old Henry VIII died after divorcing two wives and chopping off the heads of another two, he was succeeded by his elder daughter, Mary, who had steadfastly remained a Roman Catholic. The first thing that Mary did on becoming Queen was to mount a revengeful campaign against all the senior clergy appointed by her father. She became known as Bloody Mary but probably Barbecue Mary might have been a more suitable term as she loved to burn her hapless victims at the stake.

Tyburn became the Londoner's favourite entertainment spot as they queued up to witness these unfortunate burnt offerings frizzling away in the name of a god. On certain days you could probably get a three burnings offer for the price of two.

Mary was succeeded by her young brother Edward. He didn't live long enough to do too much damage, but when Elizabeth the First came to the throne she lost very little time in chopping heads, this time it was the Protestants carrying out their reign of terror.

This conflict carried on for many years in England. It waned as the British became more interested in converting the "natives" overseas or playing football, but the conflict bitterly persisted in Ireland until only recently and is still a problem in parts of Scotland.

I remember one appalling incident during the recent "troubles" in Ireland, where members of one faction stopped a bus. The people on the bus were invited to alight from the bus. If they were of the opposing faction they were shot immediately, the others were allowed to live. The same thing happened in Iraq more recently when there was an identical incident between Sunni and Shi'ite factions. I can't remember which faction did the shooting and which faction got shot. It is not really important as it could easily have been done either way. All in the name of God.

Like many thousands of returning servicemen, I found it very hard to get used to civilian life. I found domestic life particularly difficult. I had grown used again to having plenty of buddies around me. I went to Cornwall. I lived in a hostel and worked on several farms. The work was hard and gruelling but it was good for me.

I got well in with one farmer and he let me use a bell tent in one of his fields. My mother's tiny legacy had been collected and I toyed with the idea of buying a snack bar in the lovely village of Porthleven. But then I developed a nasty abcess in my right hand. I couldn't work so I decided to go back to Liverpool and impose myself once again on poor Aunt Joan. For a while I dabbled in making and selling fishcakes, any sort of edible food was welcome at the time. I applied for a Purser's job with Cunard. They were interested, and I fancied myself on the great queen liners, going to and from New York chatting up film stars. They told me to come back in three months when I had learned to type. So I did, but then I met Sylvia. I was twenty-three, she was twenty-seven. I had improved on my early groping with Rose but I never really felt comfortable with the opposite sex. This time, I was smitten. Sylvia was the first girl I ever met who I could talk to easily, she was also very pretty. So the sea-going life was out. I was about to be domesticated. I applied for a job as

Executive Trainee with the Dunlop Rubber Company.
Sounded good. It wasn't.

The problem with the god business is that there are hundreds of other different beliefs or isms all claiming their god is the one and only true god. Apart from Christianism, there is Hinduism, Sikhism, Judaism, Voodooism, some you daren't even mention for fear of being bumpedoffism, Confucianism, Buddhism, Jehovah's Witnessism.

And there are still relatively new ones springing up. Like Mormonism, sorry I forgot about that. God did actually spake to an American guy called Joe Smith round about 1830 and gave him a whole chapter of revelations which were based on the teachings of Christ. Joe was also told that it was OK to have up to five wives, or was it six, but that soon became an option rather than a clear instruction. Maybe Joe could deal with six wives but most of his followers couldn't cope, which is hardly surprising. But polygamy still remains an option apparently. He was also told that tobacco, alcohol, coffee, tea and fizzy drinks were all forbidden, which is quite a good idea if you want to be healthy but doesn't do a lot for one's social life.

An even more recent religion is Scientologyism. New religions are called cults by the way, they have to survive for at least a hundred years before they warrant being called a religion. I have struggled to come to grips with what Scientologyism is about. I gather it has something to do with aliens who came to the earth and inhabited certain people's souls, but I'm not sure. But leading intellectuals such as Tom Cruise and John Travolta are followers. Come on, now, these people are superstars, there must be something in it.

But then, if some young fellow, preferably with a beard and sandals, turned up tomorrow and claimed to be born of a virgin and said he was the son of God and that if you did as he asked then you would have eternal life, well that would be a cult. But if he got enough people to believe his revelations, after a hundred years or so it could become a religion.

There are some people on a Pacific Island, near the Philippines I think, who honestly believe that their god is the Duke of Edinburgh, our very own Prince Philip, and one day he will visit them and give out some goodies. This is a true story, but I wouldn't bet on the Duke of Edinburgh handing out goodies.

I have been without religious faith since reading Thomas Paine's "Age of Reason" at the age of fifteen. So I thought the best thing to do with life was to help towards founding a Paradise on earth.

When I was seventeen, I became a convinced Communist. It seemed like a good idea to a callow, idealistic youth. I liked the phrase "From each according to his abilities, to each according to his needs". It sounded good at the time, but the system doesn't, regrettably, fit in with the bit of blob background which we have inherited.

I used to attend meetings and rallies and I remember being really excited about going to a meeting where the great scientist Professor J B S Haldane was to be the main speaker. To my astonishment he opened his address with a quotation from the Bible: "Wherein lies a man's heart, therein lies his treasure." There's a bit of self-interest for you. He went on to explain that as a scientist there would be greater funds available for him under a Communist regime. He was probably right, but what about the starving comrades? Well, they would possibly benefit in the long run, in the meantime Professor Haldane would have a ball spending large amounts of government money indulging his love of scientific research. What a selfish comrade.

So trying to build a heaven on Earth didn't work. In fact it was a huge failure in human and economic terms. The Eastern European ex-Communist bloc countries are still recovering from over fifty years of wasted opportunity under their dreary regimes. Now Britain is invaded by thousands of their citizens trying to earn a decent living whereas what they should be doing is staying at home helping to rebuild their fragile economies. So, no heaven on earth under communism.

If you tell people you work in the Rubber Industry, they sometimes tend to roll their eyes in a lascivious way. I can assure you there is nothing sexy about rubber. When I started with Dunlop at their Walton works I was put in the Mill Room where the raw rubber is mixed. There was a strong smell and I would go home every night feeling sick. This persisted all week. On the following Monday I thought I would give it one more try before giving up the job. But I felt OK. We blobs are adaptable.

I spent six months working for a period in all the departments and offices and enrolled for an evening course in Rubber Technology. At the end of that period I was offered a job in a new latex foam factory based in Hirwaun, near Aberdare in South Wales. The factory made the well-known Dunlopillo brand and I was offered the job of Head of the Inspection Department. Starting with a small team of about ten we went from nothing to full capacity within twelve months, making mattresses and cushioning for the car and furniture industries. A rented house went with the job if you were married. Sylvia and I had intended to get married anyway, so on July 29th 1950 I married Sylvia Margaret Morris by special licence. The registrar thought Sylvia was pregnant so he was very snooty, but this was not to happen until six years later.

We set up our first little home in a post-war pre-fabricated bungalow. Life was wonderful. We worked hard but we made good friends. I have always liked the South Welsh people, they are very friendly and open. I began to dabble in amateur theatre, not always of the highest standard. But I learnt from my mistakes. Then I met a young English graduate, Lyndon Harries. He had a passion for drama and was a pretty good actor. Between us we recruited some friends and formed the Cambrian Players. Aberdare was blessed with a wonderful 800-seater theatre, the Coliseum. We opened there with the farce "Dry Rot". It packed them in. We decided we would present four plays a year and we did. Shakespearian productions included Othello, Twelfth Night, King Lear. Other plays were The Miser, Ring Round the Moon, The Hostage, Billy Liar, The Glass Menagerie, All my Sons, Death of a Salesman and many others. One year we excelled ourselves by winning the International Festival of Drama at the Prince of Wales theatre, Cardiff, with a production of "The Long and the Short and the Tall". Wonderful years.

On the home front, Sylvia presented me with two beautiful children. Helen was the first. When she was brought home from the hospital, I would sit and watch in her tiny crib, marvelling at each little movement. What a wonder. Our son Ian was born at home. I was called from work at 3pm and I popped into the local shop to get the midwife a box of chocolates. "Have you heard the news" I said excitedly. "Yes," she replied, "Isn't it terrible". I learned later that the young Busby Babes of Manchester United had been killed in an air crash on the same day.

Helen and Ian both spent their toddling days in South Wales. Everybody would stop and talk to them, they were good days. But things were not too good on the work front. There was fierce competition from new companies, easily beating our prices. The great cumbersome Dunlop machine reacted too slowly. I found a job in Streatham, South London and with a mixture of sadness and hope we moved to London in August 1963. Not long after I left the mighty Dunlop company collapsed. Well, I kept telling them my salary was inadequate.

10

The After-Life

So you've been a good boy or a good girl all your life. Now it's time to go to the Paradise of your ancient faith. Just imagine Henry who has been married to Elsie for sixty years. He passes on, as they say, and three years later he is joined by Elsie. Would the conversation go something like this…?

"Hullo Henry," says Elsie, "it's wonderful to see you again. How are you?"

"Heavenly", he replies.

"Did you miss me, darling?"

"Well, its heaven, isn't it? You don't miss anything. Everything is here."

"Oh. I thought you might have missed me… just a little bit."

"No."

"Oh, I'm disappointed to hear that… it seems like a nice place anyway. What do you do here all the time?"

"There's another fucking harp concert tonight."

"Pardon?!"

"If I hear another harp I shall go fucking barmy."

"Really, Henry, in sixty years of marriage, I've never heard you use language like that."

"We are encouraged to express our feelings freely… if we have any."

"What else do you do? There must be some nice things to do here."

"Well, there's bingo, but it doesn't cost anything and if you get a line up you don't get a prize because you can have anything you want anyway, so it's a bit of a non-event really. And there are beautiful parks with lakes, all sorts of lovely flowers and not a weed in sight. We sit and contemplate them… It's heavenly."

"I don't think you're very happy here," says Elsie sadly.

"Of course I'm happy, I'm in Heaven."

"Is my sister Doris up here?"

"No, I'm afraid not, she's in the other place, she's on a ten hour shift stoking boilers, but they have parties now and again, she seems quite happy there."

"But you're not, are you? You've got no-one to argue with."

"Of course I'm happy, how many times do I have to tell you? Anyway, there's nothing to argue about here because everything is sorted out."

(He sings "Heaven, I'm in heaven…". There is a pause.)

"I'm going to ask for transfer down below," says Elsie. "I reckon I'll have a better time with my sister. Goodbye."

I took up the post of Quality Manager with P B Cow Ltd, a company supplying rubber parts to practically every other manufacturing unit in the UK and some plants overseas. The main building was a fine old Victorian place on the south side of Streatham Common which is now owned by Sainsbury and is a protected building. Through the years there had been added willy-

nilly a succession of wooden huts, brick buildings and other assorted constructions. The site was a mess but a hive of activity. The company manufactured a vast range of products: hoses, gaskets, seals, weather strips, bungs, grommets, plungers, complicated fabrications, hot water bottles and much more. Our customers included Hoover, Hotpoint, Fords, Volvo, British Leyland, Jaguar, Rolls Royce, the Talbot/Peugeot group, the Ministry of Defence, Boots, Glaxo and most pharmaceutical manufacturing companies. And many more smaller companies. If our production schedules were not met or there was a fault in the quality we had the potential to stop hundreds of assembly lines around the country and overseas. This did happen on occasions. A Quality Manager's nightmare. I held this job for twenty-five years from 1963 to 1988. I still have nightmares about it. But on the whole, despite all its problems, I enjoyed it. We had a really keen, lively management team. I had also previously discovered the ability to leave problems behind once I left the works. But with a new job I thought I had better give the theatre world a miss.

This abstention lasted for all of six months. There were several good drama companies in Croydon. I had the opportunity to play Vladimir, one of the tramps in Samuel Becket's masterpiece "Waiting for Godot". When I first read the text I hadn't had much idea what it was about but I realised as the rehearsals went on what a fine work it was. I then joined another company who performed a wide variety of classical and modern plays. Ten years later this led to my being offered the part-time post of Director of Croydon Youth Theatre. I will be writing about that particularly satisfying part of my life in Part Two.

My main employer, like many other manufacturers in 1988, was suffering from a shrinking market. I had worked there for twenty-five years, for the last fifteen years I was spending the evenings and most week-ends with the Youth Theatre. I must have been doing a seventy-hour week. Quite suddenly I felt exhausted. My daughter Helen had married a Welshman and they had a 12-month-old daughter, Joanne. We had visited the area where they lived and liked it very much. Sylvia wanted to be near her grandchild and I needed a change. So in October 1988 we moved to a little village near Mold. My son Ian still lives in the London area with his partner.

Meanwhile in another part of Paradise a shy young man enters. There is a lady to greet him.

"Ah, Ahmed, we've been expecting you. My name is Polly Jones. This is actually the South Wales branch of Paradise. I'm a convert, see. My 'usband thought I'd look better with a veil."

"Oh, that's nice," says Ahmed with his Bradford accent.

"How are you then, bach?"

"Well," replies Ahmed, "not too bad considering, it were quite a big bang really, still getting me bits together."

"Yes, well, our Recovery Parts Unit is very thorough, they always get it together eventually... You've just got the one little piece missing... pity it's the end of your penis, but don't worry, it'll be found and we'll slot it back in place again, nothing to worry about bach."

"Oh thank you, thank you very much."

"Now then, we promised you sixty-five maidens, didn't we?"

"Well, I thought it were seventy-five actually."

(She consults her notes.)

"Ah, yes, you're quite right. Seventy-five. Unfortunately we're having a little problem with maidens at the moment."

"Oh dear, not too serious I hope."

(Polly is slightly embarrassed but continues.)

"You see, what's happened, we've had a couple of girl bombers registered. Well this being Paradise they've started all this equal rights for women nonsense and they've demanded seventy-five young men. Well, fair dos, isn't it? Well, not surprisingly, the lads can't get their heads round the idea of being one out of seventy-five, so they've refused to co-operate. So now the maidens have refused to co-operate, so I'm afraid there's nothing doing at the moment."

"Oh dear," says Ahmed. "I were looking forward to them maidens. But it will be sorted out, will it?"

(Polly continues briskly.)

"Well, we are thinking of a policy change actually. You see, what we found was that young lads like you are not terribly experienced with young maidens, so dealing with one maiden was a problem, never mind seventy-five. Pity really, we had some really good technology going. Each young chap had a remote with three choices, he could have them fully dressed, say, if he just wanted a cup of tea, or partially dressed, or completely naked, just at the touch of a button."

"Oh, that sounds really great."

"Yes, exactly, that was just the trouble. You see, the lads weren't used to seeing young maidens uncovered, so they were jumping the gun, as it were, before they actually touched a maiden. One look and it was all over. So it took several weeks before they could manage two or three, never mind seventy-five. So the other girls weren't too happy."

(Ahmed is crestfallen.)

"Oh. I see. We weren't told about that, that's very disappointing."

(Polly is encouraging.)

"Come on now, no need to be down, it's not all bad news. Some of the more… er… the more… mature ladies have come forward to offer their services, because we mustn't forget our young heroes. Now I have an auntie who's prepared to stand in, as it were, or should I say lie in, ha ha ha… well, she's more like an elder sister really, you'd never guess her age, she's looked after herself pretty well, you know, she's filled out here and there a little bit but on the whole she's in pretty good nick. I've arranged for her to come and see you today, how will that suit you?"

(Ahmed is disconsolate.)

"Well I suppose it'll have to do. When I think of all those white slags in Bradford I've turned down it makes me feel quite bitter."

We chose to live near Mold because that was the site of Theatr Clwyd Y Cymru, then known simply as Theatr Clwyd, a very high quality theatre with an international reputation. The theatre became the main focus of my life. I attended workshops, eventually graduated to conducting the adult workshop which soon became a weekly event. The theatre also instigated workshops around the schools and I became one of their tutors. I badgered the Director of the Theatre, Toby Robertson, and anyone who would listen to me, for a part in one of their productions. I put together a one-man show based on the works of Dylan Thomas. It must have impressed somebody because I was offered a part in a play called "The Guardsman" with Jenny Seagrove and Oliver Parker and, at the age of 65, I was issued with an Equity card. I'd arrived at last. I managed to get a London agent and have since appeared in various television programmes including two very lucrative Spanish commercials. I also formed my own theatre company and toured the country, performing in various plays, seven of which I wrote myself. Happy days.

In 1991 we were blessed with a grandson, Andrew, a brother for Joanne. Sylvia took great pride and pleasure in her beloved grandchildren and enjoyed their formative years. Unfortunately she developed heart problems and after a long illness she died in 1999.

Meanwhile, in the Buddhist Department of Paradise, a large, aggressive man is greeted by a polite but efficient, business-like lady.

"Ah, good morning, Mr U Thug, very pleased to meet you. It isn't every day we are able to greet a former Government Minister to Paradise. Even though you were at one time part of the despotic government of Burma, you did eventually realise your vicious ways and become a good Buddhist monk. I am sure that the people you have murdered or thrown in gaol have also found

Paradise. But we recognise you did go some way to redeeming yourself."

"Oh, yes, thank you. I am truly penitent."

"Good… very good… splendid… although as you must know our religion insists on a measure of down-grading if one's behaviour has not been… satisfactory. Well now, let's get straight to the point. Reincarnation. This will be your fifteenth, according to our records. You have had some very different and interesting lives. But the last time you really did get above yourself you know, didn't you now?"

"Look, I've already told you I have repented all that. Don't try and teach ME the meaning of humility."

"Not at all. Humility. Splendid. So we've got something really humble for you. I'm sure you are going to enjoy it."

"Oh," replies U Thug, "I do hope so. What is it?"

"An earth worm. Now now, don't be disheartened, it won't be a disabled earth worm, you understand, we won't impose disabilities on you… not yet… no, no, a perfectly capable earth worm. It can be a very useful existence, you aerate the soil, you get to know the other earthworms, who can be very jolly creatures, and if you finish up as a bird's breakfast you might make another quick re-appearance up here."

(U Thug is indignant.)

"Well, I hardly think that is a suitable existence for an intellectual person like me…"

"Now, now, don't get hoity toity, just remember we're all God's creatures. You know the rules, you weren't so intellectual when you were beheading all those people or beating them up in gaol…"

"Listen, I've already told you I've repented all that."

"True, that's all in your favour although your manner doesn't quite reflect that. But an earth worm's not a bad existence you know, it's nature right at the bottom of the heap… and there's lots of other worms you can debate the meaning of life with. I know it's dark but you'll have some good healthy minerals about you. Why not give it a try?"

(U Thug is emphatically shaking his head.)

"I see, so you refuse. Well, as you know, you have already used up two of your refusals. If you find yourself with no refusals left you could finish up being something awful like a literary critic panning a brilliant work like this."

"Well, I suppose I have to confess I have done some bad things in my past, but I couldn't stoop to that."

"Well now, that shows good discernment. Now let's just see if I might have something else."

(She fiddles very importantly on her computer.)

Ah yes, something's just come up here… a very cuddly Persian cat… and it is for someone really special… some sexy Hollywood actress… she's called Jennifer Lopez… she likes to have a cat on her lap and stroke him."

"I'll take it," says U Thug with a wild gleam.

And so U Thug, an ill-bred man, became a well-bred cat.

I hate to sound churlish but no one ever seems to remember the previous lives they have lived. Surely that's a bit odd to say the least.

In the year 2000 I got in my old car and went for a long drive through France and Spain. Arriving back in

England, I mooched about in Croydon with old friends and realised how miserable it was to live on one's own. A mutual friend introduced me to a lively, loving lady called Jean. She too had been widowed after her husband's long illness and she had worked in the film industry for nearly all her working life. We were married in March 2003 on the day the Iraq war began. But I'm pleased to record that our marriage has been happy and peaceful. She loved living in North Wales after the hustle and bustle of London and readily assumed the mantle of sound and lighting operator for our small company. So far we have done four productions together. These included presenting two plays on a cruise liner which we were invited to repeat on five additional cruises. We have recently moved permanently to France where we intend to live happily ever after.

Part Two

1

Secular Laws please, in a civilising world

The Archbishop of Canterbury, who I am sure is a very nice chap who wants to please everyone, recently submitted that some parts of Islamic Law, Sharia, would "unavoidably" be adopted in Britain. He went on to say that the Christian Doctrine states God exists as the Father, the Son and the Holy Spirit and conflicts with Islamic teaching that there is one all-powerful God. He goes on to say that some Muslims find this Christian belief difficult, sometimes offensive. He continues by saying "what we need to break the current cycles of violence is to show the world that faith and faith alone can truly ground a commitment to peace".

What I find offensive is that, in the light of knowledge we have in the 21st Century, we should even consider basing our laws on any religion. As for any kind of compromise, the basis of all religions is "Thou shalt have no other god but me". The dear old Church of England has always been flexible in its beliefs, but I doubt if you will get our Muslim or Roman Catholic or Jewish friends to move one inch from their authoritarian beliefs. As for faith grounding a commitment to peace, faith seems rather to have achieved the exact opposite effect in many conflicts in the past.

No, our laws should be based on fairness and justice, our morals should be based on sensible behaviour, honesty and integrity not any dogma of doubtful validity. They should also apply to all British citizens.

I agree that a faith or religion offers hope that a better life awaits believers and the promise that they may be reunited with their loved ones. But if it is all a delusion, as it very probably is, then what use is that? We must live in this world and do the best we can.

I also agree that religion also offers a code of conduct by which one lives one's life. But blind faith and a belief in doubtful dogma is not necessary or desirable to develop a set of rules by which to live one's life.

We can make our own rules. So Speaks The Gospel of Harry.

Because the human animal on its evolutionary journey has developed a conscience, and a group way of living, we all instinctively know the fundamentals of what is "right" or "wrong" in our own minds. Take away the god bit from the Ten Commandments and the rules are almost there.

Cynics may say: "Ah well, we only have one life, and it's a short life, there's no damnation or salvation, so let's follow our early blob instincts to survive, to be number one, self-seeking, self-indulgent, get out of my way you sorry, inferior creature." Of course, there are people like that, but there are also many people who have no religion at all, but as soon as you meet them you know they are essentially good people. I'm not implying that religious people are not well-meaning or good people. I'm simply protesting that we heretics should also stake our claim to the Moral High Ground. Why can't we be good too? Besides, this would mean standing up straight instead of grovelling on our knees.

So how do we begin the climb to the giddy heights of this moral high ground? And how do we get maximum fulfilment, enjoyment or happiness (or whatever you like to call it) on this Earth of ours?

Most of us know the ground rules already but I would like to clarify my own views in the hope that they may be of interest to younger people and hopefully even their parents. I would say that before you start giving out free advice on how other people should live their lives, you should have a good idea of how to run your own life. Not necessarily rich, but possessing a fair degree of self-reliance and experience of the way of the world.

2

Good parenting and nurturing

We have a huge element of parasitic behaviour in our midst. Before we can make any kind of moral judgements we are obliged firstly to make some contribution to society by our work and our behaviour.

So-called "benefits" are simply freebies handed out from taxes paid by those who work. These should be reserved for people who really need them, such as the chronically ill or the disabled.

One of our former Prime Ministers Benjamin Disraeli famously remarked that there are "lies, damned lies and statistics". So I do not wish to go into statistics. But it is generally agreed that there are large numbers of young people aged sixteen to twenty-five who have never worked. Furthermore, one glance at many of these young people from a prospective employer would have him shaking his head with a firm "No, thank you". There are also large numbers who work only occasionally and large numbers of people on Tax-payers' money who claim to be chronically sick or disabled who are in fact only suffering from "sicknoteitis".

When I say large numbers, I mean millions.

Work is good for the individual, for his family and his country. Not working is going against your blob ancestry. We are born to forage and feather the nest.

In the animal world most offspring have a male and female parent who would fight to the death to protect their young. I believe that every child needs two parents, thus providing a female influence and a male influence.

Nowadays couples may decide to live together, they may not marry, after a while they may choose to separate. They may then live alone or they may decide on another partner. This is perfectly acceptable and is in accordance with the Natural Selection theory of Evolution; that is, your blob background. And we do live in a free society. Don't we?

Well, not entirely, because with freedom and the civilising process comes responsibilities. We cannot rob, pillage, rape, throw litter, drive above the speed limits, libel, slander, kill, kick dogs, urinate in public, smoke tobacco in public places, commit arson… the list is endless. Most laws are sensible; those which are of doubtful benefit should be thoroughly debated.

But the Gospel of Harry says that once the woman conceives, a marriage or civil contract should bind them together, a contract which should ensure that couples stay together until the child is at least eighteen. Not too long ago this process was called a shotgun wedding.

Childless marriages or partnerships may be easily ended as they are now, but once a child is born a separation or divorce should be granted only under exceptional circumstances such as insanity or the use of violence. Every child needs and is entitled to a father and a mother, and this should be accepted by parents with joy and understanding. This is essential, paramount to an orderly civilised society.

The Gospel of Harry states that Family Allowances should be withheld until this contract of care is signed and agreed. If a couple are not prepared to agree with this, then they can either not have children or forfeit child allowances. There are reliable contraceptives available. If you must be a Roman Catholic, opt out of their birth control policy. Don't worry, millions are already doing it. Don't buy a puppy for Christmas and don't beget a child just for a couple of months or a couple of years. It is for life, or at least until the offspring is able to fend for itself. This way thousands of other tax-payers are assured that they do not have to pay for the upbringing of someone else's child, but more importantly it is in the child's best interest. Various attempts have been made over the year to secure payment from deserting parents, which have been largely unsuccessful. This is hardly surprising. How can'the average person possibly support two households? Multiple divorces with dependent children can only be afforded by film-stars, Arab sheiks, premiership footballers or business tycoons.

I already hear the chorus of disapproval from those who think it is better that children should not have to live with parents who quarrel with each other. This is nonsense, what parents with children do not quarrel? Remember that fathers, mothers and children all have animal instincts. They have to do the best they can and advance their progress to a better civilisation. Families are only really continuously happy on phoney sanitised commercials, everyone smiling, laughing with synthetic jollity. Real life isn't like that. But family life is a good foundation and can be good. But you need to work at it. Many couples with children give up on their marriages too easily nowadays. Children are left with a feeling of abandonment. And then children also have to come to terms with step-fathers or a continuing procession of "Uncles" as they are sometimes called. It is not uncommon these days for a child to have up to five step-fathers.

Whilst some children have a very bad start in life, at the other end of the scale there are children who are so cosseted and spoiled that when they come to adult life they are unable to cope with not having anything they want at the click of the fingers. These conditions can apply to all classes of people. There is much talk of "child poverty" these days. Most child poverty is caused by people who have too many children, or mothers (or sometimes fathers) who are abandoned by their spouses and above all by parents who won't work. On the other hand, many children's bedrooms are so full of computer games, toys and televisions that there is hardly sufficient room for the bed.

Many young women refer to marriage as the biggest and most important day in their lives. They are wrong. The most important day in a man or woman's life is the day they become a parent.

I do not need to say that having a child is one of the most wonderful experiences that one can have in life. I remember gazing at my newly born children with wonder. I would just watch them for hours at a time; even a tiny yawn or a little stretch would seem like a miracle. And later on I would marvel at the steady unflinching gaze, the first enchanting smile and the first doddering, uncertain steps. Like little kittens and little puppy dogs they can win your hearts completely. Of course, they do cry sometimes during the night, or let's face it, more than sometimes, and they do get up to mischief, but one has to accept that as being part of the joy of parenthood. When my daughter was about 18 months old her favourite pastime was peeling off wallpaper. I won't even mention what my son got up to.

But they've both grown up reasonably civilised.

But the parent also has to understand that a little animal has been brought into the world.

Like all blobs, children see themselves as the centre of the Universe and believe that everything is designed specifically for them. The first instinct of the child is to do it 'my way', which if unchecked can prove disastrous. It is no use to talk about children starving in Ethiopia when all they want is a Milky Way.

But what is worse than a spoiled child? From our humble protoplasmic origins we should be striving to further the civilisation process. An important part of this process is to demonstrate that the child can't have every thing it wants. A parent must learn how to say a clear, unwavering 'no', loud and often.

In certain areas of our country we are regressing; that is, the evolutionary process of civilisation is being reversed. This is almost entirely due to children who have either been spoiled or neglected and have grown into horrible little brats who develop into selfish, perhaps even dangerous adults. Some may even kick you to death outside your own doorstep just for the fun of it, although the current fashion is to stab you with a knife. They also become unfit to become parents.

Children have to be loved and nurtured, but they also have to realise that they are not the centre of the world and firstly, there are other people to be considered. They need both a mother and a father, a male and a female influence.

This is not just a grumpy old man speaking. The public of all ages are now speaking openly about "a broken society". The remedy is simple. It is simply a matter of bringing up children properly. I make haste to add that many parents are doing this already, let us learn therefore from them.

Both parents should make sensible rules and keep to them. The earlier you start the better. As they grow larger, children's destructive powers become greater. In doing this you will be doing your children the greatest favour. Contrary to popular belief, children love rules, they then know exactly how they stand. Channel their energies and enthusiasm into suitable interests. Don't let them gaze at the television or stare boggle-eyed into a computer all day. And do not allow the children to become the all-consuming reason for parents' existence. A little bit of neglect can work wonders sometimes. Never talk down to children, talk to them as young adults, reward them in some small way for good behaviour.

Parents should have lives and interests too and you will find that children will appreciate and accept that. Can there be anything more boring than parents talking constantly about their darling little children? Be proud of them, certainly. And above all, lead. You are in charge, they are dependent on you. Nowadays adults almost seem to apologise for being parents, they may quickly become fuddy-duddies in their children's eyes. Especially when the child becomes adolescent. Have none of that. You are the leaders in your home.

But enjoy them. Bringing up a family to the best of your abilities should be a joy. It's easy to talk but it's true.

Some perceptive chap said, anarchy starts when the old fail to control the young. This is happening too often.

Schoolteachers have to deal with huge problems of indiscipline. How long will it be before the education system becomes unworkable? Discipline in school requires immediate attention, but it starts from the home.

Let me tell you about my experience as a Youth Theatre Director. Before I became a professional actor I was involved in the Amateur Theatre. There are some very good amateur companies who set very high standards. As a result of my work on the amateur stage the Chairman of Croydon Youth Theatre invited me to become Director of that organisation. I would rather have received an offer from a successful Film or Theatre director but, nevertheless, I was flattered; at least someone thought I was passable. I was concerned that I had had no training in working with young people apart from being a parent, but I decided to accept none the less. It was initially a part time post.

This was in the early seventies. During the sixties there were great social changes, many of them for the good. It is inevitable that young people will want change, that is part of the evolutionary process, but some changes made in the sixties were disastrous. They were often based on adolescent views that they knew much better than their parents. This belief has gone on through the ages and has always and probably will always be a cause of conflict. But in the 1960s most parents seemed to abrogate all responsibilities and simply caved in.

It took everyone several years to find out how wrong both the children and the parents had been. Good manners and respect for teachers and authority all but disappeared. Many of our young people were revolting in every sense of the word. And we are still suffering from it today. Misguided rules and regulations gradually followed, which stripped teachers, parents and the local bobbies of much of their authority. With the lack of discipline came a great increase in bullying. Remember, children are not little angels, they can be very, very nasty if they are not properly controlled. I speak from personal experience as I could be particularly horrid if given half a chance.

During the period of the sixties and seventies older people would say with a wry smile "I think our young people of today are wonderful" - but I suspect it was said because if they didn't join in with the current adulation of the young they thought they would be derided as being not "with it". Too many parents were too easily humiliated by this attitude.

I had seen some excellent productions staged by Croydon Youth Theatre so I was well aware of the potential talent of young people, but the group had been in decline for several years. I approached the project cautiously. I was introduced to about fifteen demoralised teenagers, about an even mixture of boys and girls. I talked to them about the activities of the group and I found to my astonishment that the group had not been given the opportunity to stage a play within the last eighteen months. If you join a football club you will have to practice throw-in and corner kicks and tactics and what-not, but you would surely also want to play a game of football on a regular basis.

So I suggested we put a show on in six weeks, a show which would involve every member and also include any new member who might come along. I was fortunate enough to be able to enlist a talented young woman colleague, Leslie Bennett, a good all-rounder who could sing, dance and act. I explained that we would have to allot more time together than the customary two evenings a week. The trend then was, I understood, to involve young people as much as possible in decision making, so I asked them whether they would prefer the extra rehearsal to be held on a Saturday or a Sunday. The response was a confused mumbling. A young girl of about fourteen tugged my sleeve.

"'Ere, arry," she said, "can I give you a piece of advice?"

I accepted immediately.

"Well," she continued, "if I were you I wouldn't ask them things like that, they'll talk about it for hours. You decide yourself and tell them what you want. If there's anyone who can't make it on the day you choose, they'll tell you so."

So I chose Sunday and everyone agreed.

So there it was. My Youth Theatre training was completed in half a minute. What they were saying was, you lead and we'll follow. That doesn't simply mean you impose your ideas on them and stifle any creativity they may show. It simply means you're in charge. I had been planning to discuss with them what sort of show to do. But I'd already decided on a format, so I said "Right, let's get cracking".

In six weeks the rudimentary show went on as planned. In that period they discovered the satisfaction of working together as a team, the sheer joy of pleasing an audience, a joy which every performer knows, and the subsequent bonding of a demoralised group of youths into an enthusiastic band of young performers. Equally important, the parents were thrilled.

I did that job for fifteen years and it gave me enormous satisfaction. After a couple of years Croydon Council provided us with our own premises. Part of a disused school was converted into a 100-seater theatre and two rehearsal rooms. We called it the Shoestring Theatre because we hadn't got much money. I had always dreamed of running my own theatre. To be able to choose what plays would be produced and to progress them from initial reading to performance was a delight. We attracted young people from the age of 14 to 21 but some wouldn't leave until they were 23 or 24, and I let them stay and used their experience to help the younger members. At times the membership would be in three figures.

With the aid of three enthusiastic tutors we staged between ten and twelve plays a year. One year we did fifteen productions. We also did regular training sessions or "workshops" as they are known. I followed my own instincts and put on plays which I wanted to do, because they were worthy plays. The sages would sometimes shake their heads and say, you can't do that with kids. I proved them wrong. Young people are under-estimated. I put on plays by Shakespeare, Moliere, Arthur Miller, Tennessee Williams, Lorca, Alan Ayckbourn, Pinter, Beckett, Wesker and scores of up- and-coming new writers. We also did broad comedy, farce and musicals, including three original musicals especially written for the company. We also improvised and structured our own shows and plays. I came to treat our members as young professionals. When they took on a part they were expected to prepare properly for it. If they didn't, I replaced them. In fact I only had to do this on very rare occasions. They couldn't all be brilliant, but they had to work at it. I gained deep satisfaction from bucking the sixties' trend, if only in a small way.

We built up a solid core of support, not just from parents, but also from the parents of those members who had moved on. These were particularly supportive. Some of them would say, what a wonderful job you are doing for our young people. I never told them I was only doing it as a substitution for a career in the professional theatre. "Wherin lies a man's heart therein lies his treasure." I think I've already quoted that little gem from the Bible. I was running my own theatre! I had found my treasure. I could put on plays. Of course I did get satisfaction from helping our young members but I couldn't have done it if I hadn't wanted to. Many of our members progressed to drama schools and then to professional work. But the main objective of the group was to create and sustain interest in drama, and instil a sense of self-confidence and also experience the great joy of accomplishing something worthwhile as part of a group effort.

I never actively encouraged members to go in for theatre professionally as it must surely be one of the most competitive professions one could choose. But we have several ex-members who have made a steady living from it. Sometimes I see them on television or, better still, I see them if they are working at local theatres, and this is very satisfying. One of the greatest compliments I had was from a girl who was initially a little difficult but eventually developed into a useful member. At the age of about thirty she stopped me in the street one day and said "Thank you for being a bastard". She was quite a big wheel in the travel business. She largely attributed her success to having been a member of Croydon Youth Theatre.

Sorry about that, I got rather carried away, but I hope I've made a point. Set standards high and you get better results. Love your subject and it brushes off… well, nearly always.

During my time at the Youth Theatre I know of three girl members who had babies at an early age because they were aware that the local council would reward them with a council house or a flat, usually rent free. Have you ever heard anything so preposterous? There was a time when politicians could speak disapprovingly about single mothers. Then it became taboo to dare to criticise the young darlings. Well, let me say at once I heartily disapprove of single mothers. It is not good for the mother, it is not good for the child and it is not good for society in general. My mother was a single mother of three young boys for six years after my father died and they were very difficult years. Thus Speaks The Gospel Of Harry.

3

Sexual urges (keep calm)

The sexual drive is a huge part of human life. As I have said earlier, Sigmund Freud says it is the most important motivator in our lives. It comes directly from the blob. Survive and multiply, but in the civilised world only multiply when you can support the child. There is no need to feel any guilt about the sexual urge. That is the way we are. And it should be something to enjoy.

So when you reach an age when you begin to experience those exciting but disturbing urges, what are you supposed to do about it? Well, the Gospel of Harry is not a Sex Manual but I can offer a simple solution.

For the young male the main thing is not to get the girl pregnant, or "get the girl into trouble" as we used to say. But to a healthy young boy a pretty girl can be very exciting, so if the feeling is mutual, you may kiss her, fondle her, embrace her - but on no account should you penetrate her with your sperm-shooter. Keep that little devil out of the no-go area until you are both of an age to deal with the consequences.

For the young girl the important thing is to enjoy his attention if you like him, but do not let the boy penetrate you. That is forbidden territory. If one of his sperm meets one of your eggs it's nappies at dawn for the next two years and baby-sitting for the next ten years. Simply say no. Never mind if the boy has a condom or not, the answer remains a firm no. If the boy doesn't respect that, you shouldn't want to know him any more.

So there you are, a simple solution. Failure to comply means that you are bound twenty-four hours a day, seven days a week, 365 days a year for many years to come to tend to a demanding expanding little bundle of mischief, which you are ill-equipped to deal with, particularly if you are without a responsible partner.

The problem of unwanted pregnancies has increased over the last ten years which may partly be due to the demon drink. Young males have always tended to over-indulge in booze. But now it seems that girls too have to get plastered before they can enjoy themselves. So if you must drink alcohol to excess, get it fixed deep down in your psyche. Always say no.

In fact, my young life was dominated by girls just saying no. That was not just me but the majority of my fellow peers. The girl said no, not just because of social disapproval but mainly because there was no financial provision for pregnant teenage girls. They were on their own.

But be assured that thousands of previous generations, including my own, have had great fun and pleasure with the opposite sex just by following the simple rule. No penetration with the sperm-shooter. There are ways of giving pleasure to each other without actually having intercourse. If you don't know how that is done I'm sure your teachers or your parents, or perhaps an older friend will tell you how. As I say, this is not a Sex Manual, in any case I'm only just getting the hang of it myself.

So girls and boys, young men and young women enjoy your love life without guilt. But when you judge the time to be right to become a parent, be responsible.

The British have the highest rate in Europe for teenage pregnancies. Don't allow yourself to get caught in that trap. Young people need time to sort out their futures before they undertake the huge responsibility of becoming parents. Fortunately most young people are sensible enough to know all this and apply their common sense.

But I wrote earlier about young girls being rewarded for having babies. As I have said, I personally know three young girls who purposely had babies as they thought it would be a good idea to get away from their parents and be given a nice new council flat.

The Gospel of Harry says if a girl under the age of eighteen has a child, that child should be the responsibility of the girl's and the boy's parents until the mother of the child reaches eighteen. There should be no family allowance paid by the Government and the child's provision should be shared by both sets of grandparents and by the young parents themselves.

That ruling would bring us down the European League of teenage pregnancies in no time at all.

There used to be three social classes in Britain. The upper class were landowners, sometimes with inherited titles, the middle classes were professional people such as lawyers, doctors and teachers, and the working classes provided the muscle and their labour for the physical work. With the advent of technology and the introduction of better social amenities, these divisions are fading into obscurity. Now, we have two classes. Those who work and those who don't work.

The last twenty-five years have seen a massive increase in an underclass of people who have got used to handouts from the government. There has recently been an influx of half a million people from Poland and other Eastern European countries. To their credit they have easily slipped into jobs and appear to work hard at them. Why, then, are we still paying unemployment benefits to our own people who reportedly can't find work? Because, regrettably, these people would rather stay at home and live "on the social".

If you can find time to look at the Jeremy Kyle or the Tricia Goddard television show, you will find it worth the effort. Three minutes is all you need to see the sheer horror of these programmes. I will give credit to them for one thing. The people who come on their shows certainly reflect this particular branch of our society with depressing accuracy. They are way down the evolutionary scale, frighteningly close to their blob instincts which are only focussed on the 'me, me, me' brute method of survival.

Here's a typical item from one of their "shows". Tracy has four children by four different fathers, but she is now pregnant with Kevin. She loves Kevin to bits but Kev is not certain that he is the father of the expected child. He already has two children of his own by some other unfortunate woman, and he has heard that his brother Wayne has been nipping into the toilet to have sex with Tracy. Wayne, who doesn't shave and has tattoos, shakes his head vigorously in denial. Their tormentor (either Jeremy or Trish, depending on which channel you are watching) relentlessly cross-examines them with inane questions:

"How could you do this to your brother, Wayne?"

"Kevin, would you still love Tracy if Wayne were found to be the father of her child?"

"Tracy, you were seen going into the toilet with Wayne by your mother-in-law Dawn on several occasions, why did you do that?"

"I never, that's not true, she's a liar..."

"She's never really liked me..."

"Tracy, is it true you have a drink problem?"

"Well, I've had a drink now and again, no more than anyone else..."

"Your mother-in-law tells me that when she calls to see you, you are nearly always drunk..."

"Well, I've told you, she's a liar..."

"Is it true, Kevin, that you are a drug user?"

"Not at all..."

"You've never taken drugs?"

"No, that's not true..."

"That's not what Wayne tells me..."

"Wayne's a liar."

"Would you be willing, Tracy, to submit to a DNA test to see who is the father of your child?"

Tracy shrugs her massive shoulders. Commercial break. High drama.

"Tracy... the father of your child is... [dramatic pause... more dramatic pause... now boring pause] ... Kevin."

Tracy, Kevin and Wayne hug each other ecstatically. Dawn makes a two finger sign and storms off. Audience claps hysterically. I resist the urge to vomit.

The gospel of Harry deplores such a way of life but recognises their right to live as they please, provided they fund their activities or lack of activities themselves. But this is not the case. The taxpayer is robbed and government revenue is robbed of money which could be put to much better purposes. And their undisciplined children run riot. These people need help and strong guidance and quickly.

I award "The Hypocrite of the Decade Award" to be jointly shared by Jeremy Kyle and Tricia Goddard. Their hypocrisy in purporting to help the undeveloped blobs who appear on their programmes is shameful. All they do is highlight their inadequacies before an equally moronic, self-righteous audience. The only thing I admire about these two people is their income.

I am aware, of course, that many rich people carry on with this self-centred self-indulgence, but at least they pay for it themselves. But a rich person has to impose self-discipline. Most of them do, that is how they became rich. It's the rich heirs and heiresses who often become the playboys or playgirls. What would we do without the inspiring intellectualism of Paris Hilton?

4

Hi Ho, Hi Ho, it's off to work we go
– all of us

The evolutionary process and the knowledge that we are descended from wild animals is illustrated by the preceding chapter. Men and women are born to forage, to provide for themselves and their offspring, to hunt and to gather and to constantly be on the look-out for danger. Take away their need to fend for themselves and they falter. Everybody must be brought back into the fold.

Again, the answer is simple. Stop all the long-term unemployment benefits and strictly re-examine the disability benefits. Work is good for one's self-esteem. Even so-called menial and repetitive tasks can be therapeutic. If I have worries, a morning working in the garden can do wonders, all problems come into perspective. When I was employed as a Quality Manager, I was beset frequently by problems. I used to go and work a machine for an hour, this would clear the mind wonderfully. Some physical work is good for everybody. There is a great snobbery in the Western world about how one earns one's living. All honest work should be valued. Hard-working men and women are the salt of the earth. And physical labour keeps you in touch with the best of your blob ancestry. Stopping long-term benefits would be the greatest service you could do for the people who are on them.

Read or go and see Arthur Miller's play "Death of a Salesman", one of the most discerning plays of the Twentieth Century. The main character, Willie Loman, an unsuccessful salesman, has grand illusions about his ability. He boasts about his prowess as a salesman, how he "knocked 'em dead" in every town and city. In reality, he's a failure. He has also great ambitions for his son Biff. During the play it becomes apparent that Willie is happiest when he is mending his front porch and Biff's idea of fulfilment is working outdoors with the sun on his back.

The Gospel According to Harry says every able-bodied person should work.

5

Education, the cornerstone of civilisation

So, that's few problems solved already. The new-broom government of 1997 was going to solve these problems. But they bottled out of it. Their Great Leader also mentioned his main policy would be education, education, education, which has resulted in failure, failure, failure. You may quote all the statistics you want but if you want to find out how bad our system is, simply talk to a teacher. They will tell you that they spend most of their time trying to keep order and dealing with disruptive children and, often, aggressive parents. Head Teachers and their staffs are professional people who are not allowed to carry out their duties as they would wish. To add insult to injury, they are bombarded daily with interfering, impractical instructions from government ministers and officials.

A most telling conversation I had was with two teachers, a married couple who had taught for five years in this country and had then gone out to Hong Kong to teach. Returning after three years for some home leave, I asked them how they liked teaching out there. Their faces lit up. They told me that back home, they spent the first twenty minutes of a one hour period trying to get a semblance of order. In Hong Kong they merely went in, said Good Morning to the class and proceeded to teach.

So, how do we begin to improve our education system?

Firstly, schools are just too big. Some of them have over 2000 pupils. It must be very intimidating for a child of eleven going to a place like that for the first time. It must take a child half a term just to find its way about. Bewildering.

So, as a matter of urgency, they should be made smaller. I am much in favour of the voucher system where groups of parents in a local neighbourhood get together and try and muster an agreed number of children. This is not a new idea but a very good one in my opinion. As a temporary measure the enormous existing schools should be split into smaller units, but separate premises should be found as a matter of urgency. For a secondary school, from ages 11 to 16, I would suggest that 250 children would be about the right number, that is 50 pupils per academic year, 25 pupils per class.

All school should be secular. Religious activity, if desired, should be outside the school.

By virtue of their reduced size, they will be local.

They should be managed by a Head Teacher and overseen by a Board consisting of Head, Administrator, a parent from each academic year, a local councillor and say four or five interested, intelligent men or women. There would be a need for twelve teachers who would cover a range of subjects. There should be an annual inspection to assess the effectiveness of the school carried out by ex-teachers with professional or business experience.

There is apparently (or there could be) a sum of money allocated by the Government to each child of educational age. These could be issued in the form of vouchers. If the value of the voucher is agreed at x pounds per person, then the revenue of the school would be to the value of x multiplied by 250. Primary schools should be restricted to 100 pupils.

Existing Grammar Schools and Independent schools should be treasured and not subject to niggling class-conscious regulations. After all, most of the well-healed "socialists", including government ministers, send their children to private schools, in spite of their "principles". At the moment we still rely on these schools to supply the best education. We must not hinder them. But the objective should be to bring the State-funded schools up to standard so that most parents would be content to send their children to them.

As the smaller "voucher" schools progress, many of the fee-paying schools will simply merge into the new system.

It is essential that schools must not be "faith" schools. They should be secular. Any unproven, ancient superstitions such as religions should be practised outside of schools if one's prejudices are deeply rooted. In any case, religions are divisive. Our aim must be to continue the progress of civilisation and minimise tribal divisiveness and religious dogma.

How wonderful it would be if in every school each pupil knew all the other pupils, knew all the teachers and probably a large proportion of the parents. Everyone would have a sense of belonging to the school and, more importantly, the school belonging to them. Just imagine it. Discipline would be much easier to enforce and the whole neighbourhood could be involved. Children can often be cocooned in their large schools in their own little world. Local residents, particularly retired ones with time on their hands, could talk to the pupils about their experiences of worlds which are often unseen or unheard by children. This would also make many retired people feel useful. The internet is a wonderful educational help but real life experiences are even better.

It is fair to recognise that some comprehensive schools are very successful, but they are simply too big. We should all applaud those who have done relatively well. Most of our teachers are doing a very difficult job under difficult, in many cases impossible, circumstances. We can still be proud of the majority of our young people, who grow up to be worthy citizens, mainly due to good parenting and good teaching. But our results compare unfavourably with the developed countries around the world and indiscipline is rife.

But growing up isn't just passing exams. It is also a matter of pressing forward the development of the human animal into a still more civilised animal. This entails consideration for one's fellows and one's elders.

Again, the Gospel of Harry has a very simple answer to this. The first step to civilisation is to simply be courteous and well-mannered. Good manners spread. It is said there is a cost and a price for everything. Good manners cost nothing. The act of common courtesy to one's fellows has diminished. It should be fully restored as soon as possible. At the very least we could stop dropping litter. That would be an enormous step forward for civilisation.

Local and National Government interference in schools should be kept to the absolute minimum. Standards should be set by professional educationalists and, in many cases, prospective employers. Education should be carried out by professionals overseen by local people elected to a Board of Governors. The Head Teacher and staff should be given full support over discipline which is almost non-existent at the moment. Let them be differing, vibrant places. They should not be managed by anonymous officials in Whitehall or governments who are more interested in social engineering. Teach knowledge, skills, a good grasp of the English language, how to speak clearly and lucidly, basic mathematics and instil civilised behaviour. Disruptive pupils should not be tolerated and should be banished to Special schools where they can be bombarded with "tough love". Periodic attendance by parents of disruptive parents should be included in the bombardment. Special Needs schools for children with genuine learning difficulties should be well-funded and managed with loving care.

It is pertinent to realise, however, that education has been wasted on certain people. They have not been able to come to terms with it, but have nevertheless turned out to be very successful in later life. Albert Einstein was told by his teacher to stop dreaming and gazing out of the window; Thomas Edison, the great inventor, had very little formal education; Winston Churchill himself writes that he was a "duffer" at Harrow School and Anthony Hopkins also writes of an aimless youth spent moping about. There are many other successful people who will also tell you that they learnt nothing at school, they even boast about it. But unfortunately the terrible fact is that there are still children who come out of school who cannot read or write or do simple sums. We must always remember that education is a process which carries on throughout every day of one's life. Incidentally, the Book of Harry knows a simple way of teaching children to read fluently by the age of four or five. I will explain later.

One of the problems nowadays is the aspirations of young people. Recent polls taken show that the large majority of children want to be rock stars, television presenters, models, film-stars or "celebrities" of some kind. Well, good luck to them, but easy options are hard to come by. The words "celebrity "and "star" in the context of achievement should be treated with caution or even eliminated. Think of the no-brainers who come out of the Big Brother programme. What is there to celebrate about them?

There is a great story about Arturo Toscanini, the late, great orchestral conductor who was having a spot of bother with a well-known opera singer. He had cause to gently rebuke her. The lady immediately protested: "You cannot speak to me like that, I am a star." Toscanini replied: "Madam, the only stars I know are in the heavens, we are merely musicians striving to do our best."

There is nothing wrong with ambition or aspirations, indeed they are to be encouraged, but one firm fact a young person has to realise is that if you want to achieve anything you have to work at it. Of course you might win the Lottery. Check with your Maths teacher the odds on that. Pretty long I'm afraid.

No, I'm afraid you've got to work at it. But work can be satisfying. But young people also have to realise that all jobs have an element of repetition. Even brain surgeons can be heard muttering "Oh, no, not another frontal lobe, I've done three already this week."

There is a wonderful line from a play by Barrie Keeffe who writes about poor kids from the East End. A pupil who thinks his education has been neglected because of teachers concentrating on the brighter children, holds two teachers as hostages and threatens to kill them. The distraught headmaster is trying to resolve the situation. He asks the boy what he wants to be in later life and swears he will help the boy to achieve that ambition. "Tell me what you want to be", he pleads.

The boy replies: "I want to be a brain surgeon… and a striker for West Ham."

One has to aspire but one has to be realistic.

It is essential that a good start be made in educational progress. This is more likely to happen if a child has the ability to read at the earliest possible stage. Being able to read opens doors to an abundance of knowledge and interest. I boasted earlier in these pages that it can be made fairly simple to teach a child to read by the age of five. Some countries believe that a child should not even start education until the age of seven. What nonsense. Mozart was writing symphonies by the age of five. Of course we can't all be Mozarts, but the human brain is a marvellous mechanism and no time should be lost in its early development.

English speakers throughout the world were denied a wonderful opportunity in 1947 when a certain Mr Follick, an MP, tried to introduce his Basic Spelling Bill. This was unanimously rejected by Parliament who were hell-bent on nationalising practically everything they could lay their hands on, thus hampering our economic recovery.

Have you ever stopped to think how ridiculous English spelling is? English is one of the most widely used languages in the world and is fast becoming the major international language in the world. So poor foreigners as well as our children have to master the contradictory rules of English spelling.

Think of the letters ough in combination. Put a b in front of them, it's pronounced bow as in bow-wow.

Put a c in front it, becomes koff.

Put an n in front and a t on the end and it becomes nought as in naughty.

Put a t on the end, it becomes ought as in haughty.

Give it a leading s and it becomes sought.

And here are two more ridiculous ones: throw an r in front and it becomes ruff, a t and it's tuff.

How did we ever learn it? Pity the poor foreigner who has to learn it. Take the word bicycle. There are two c's in the word, both have a different sound whilst the y and the i have identical sounds. And what is the e for? And why does the word 'for' have two other spellings, why fore and four to produce the same sound?

My friend Peter Dodd
has two d's but if god
is so great, it's very odd
that God has only one.

Basic phonetic spelling is not to be confused with text spelling. This is simply a kind of shorthand for sending texts by mobile phones. For those who are addicted to this practise, let them do as they will. It should on no account be adopted for everyday use.

I could go on for pages. Just take a cool, impassioned look at English spelling and you will see immediately how completely irrational it is. Some of us were convinced that decimal currency would never work. Try and explain the old currency to anyone under the age of twenty-five. You will be met with incredulous stares.

When I was a child we were taught the so-called phonetic way. Then we went on to the Look and Say method. When this was deemed a failure we reverted to the phonetic system. The trouble is, English spelling just isn't phonetic. In the English language there are five vowels, twenty consonants and the letter y which serves as a consonant and a vowel. Surely we can devise a system whereby a letter or a combination of two or occasionally three letters create one unique sound. The purists will hold up their hands in horror as they did when we went on to decimal currency. But, apart from being very easy to learn it could actually eliminate sloppy speaking where consonants are regularly dropped and words mispronounced. And a child of four would be able to read fluently.

People talk about the language of Shakespeare, forgetting that Chaucer and Spenser wrote using very different spelling from Shakespeare. English people hold their hands up in horror when they see the Welsh language in print or on road signs. Although I cannot speak Welsh I can teach a stranger to the Welsh language how to pronounce it in about ten minutes because Welsh is written almost completely phonetically.

I am sure a class of sixth-formers studying English could work out a system of phonetic spelling in one week.

This miet bee an exampel ov baysik speling;

Ay siekieatrist iz ay man hoo goes too a strip shoe and wotches the awdiens.

Which translates as:

This might be an example of basic spelling.

A psychiatrist is a man who goes to a strip show and watches the audience.

And Zed, thou unnecessary letter, as someone called it, iz sadly underuzed, iz it not?

I agree, it looks terrible at first sight but it is logical and consistent and would quickly become familiar.

The most pressing need today is that all children in this

country should have a good basic education and a good well-disciplined family to properly nurture them. The most important thing that needs to be done is to mend what is now generally accepted to be a "broken society".

Sad to relate, it may be there is a large group of people who cannot be rescued, part of a lost generation. We must almost start from the beginning again.

What we should do as a matter of urgency is double the prison capacity, so that people who kill or constantly offend with serious crimes should be locked up for a long time where every attempt must be made to rehabilitate them. There must be no procession in and out of jail because of lack of prison capacity.

And now we come to Further Education. At the time of writing the present age for leaving school is sixteen. But raising the leaving age to eighteen is, I believe, under serious consideration. I think this could be a mistake. There are many young people who have no desire to pursue an academic life; in fact, they often despise people who do have that wish. There are practical people who like to do things with their hands as well as their brains. What is wrong with that? But our present government is obsessed with social interchange, whatever that is. Boys and girls should be permitted to leave school at sixteen if they so wish.

Vocational courses are looked down upon as being inferior. What utter nonsense. There are people who want to be plumbers, carpenters, electricians, builders. The country desperately needs plumbers, carpenters, electricians, builders and other tradesmen or women.

Why do we have to have Polish plumbers? Polish plumbers should be working on Polish pipes. Is there something dishonourable about being a tradesman? There are times when we are on the phone desperately trying to get one. At such a time would you rather have a young person with a degree in Media Studies? I think not. In any case these trades can provide a good living, no need to worry about "social interchange", a good plumber can deal with that believe me.

So let us provide training grounds which can provide good occupational training, whether the compulsory leaving age is raised or not. We need them badly. Parents, teachers and governments are obsessed with universities, now diminished to the derogatory label of "uni". In an effort to increase the numbers of people attending universities, the managers of education have gone along with the introduction of useless courses in places which hardly warrant the status of universities and of technical colleges which are just an excuse for disguising the rate of unemployment.

At the same time, students are building up horrendous debts in our already debt-ridden society. Additionally, academic standards have been "dumbed down", so that an increased number of students may qualify for university entrance. Universities have soon become wise to this state of affairs.

Of course we need universities for subjects such as English, foreign languages, science, mathematics, medicine, engineering, electronics and the like, but, regrettably a university degree no longer has the status it once held.

The whole business of Further Education should be thrown in the melting pot.

Do universities really need such long holidays? The original long summer holidays from July to October were originally introduced so that the young students could go home to help their fathers with the harvests. This hardly applies today. Some courses, such as medicine and science, are very stringent and require long and systematic study. Other subjects require a great deal of reading and often students are required to attend only two or three lectures a week and these are not always compulsory. There must be many courses which can be condensed into two years.

One of the best things about university for young people is getting away from Mummy and Daddy and meeting their fellow peer groups from different areas and backgrounds. Many people look back on their National Service days in the Armed Forces during the late forties and early fifties with pleasure and gratitude as it enabled young people from various backgrounds to come together.

The Gospel of Harry states there could and should be found other ways of young people mixing together, possibly in the form of some kind of social service. The undeveloped countries, as the poverty-stricken countries are euphemistically known, need assistance to improve their living standards. Three-month courses of intensive training could be given to participants in subjects such as basic hygiene, elementary education and whatever might be recommended by those who are aware of the most urgent needs of these countries. The students, together with some experienced team leaders, could then be sent out to participating countries for an agreed period of time, say nine to twelve months. They could then work with the local people in their villages and towns, living under the local conditions. They could work on specified new projects or simply help them improve their lot. The leaders could be retired engineers, doctors or tradesmen with special skills to share and impart.

What an eye-opener that would be for many young people, many of whom are just longing to be challenged or stretched in a productive and satisfying way. They would discover the joy of helping their less fortunate brothers and sisters. Not for them the easy option of wearing a wristband saying End World Poverty, which, incidentally, I understand are made in a sweat shop in China.

How would we pay for all this, I hear you anxiously ask? Oh dear, more taxes. Not necessarily. At present the richer countries throw large amounts of money at the poorer countries. Unfortunately most poorer countries have corrupt governments and much of the money lands up in the wrong hands. This way we can see the money is being spent usefully. Global companies who benefit hugely from the natural resources of poor countries would also be happy to pay large sums of money toward such a scheme. And the young people who take part would have their lives enriched, their outlook broadened and would experience a unique sense of comradeship which would stand them in good stead for the rest of their lives. I have read that the multi-billionaire Bill Gates is leading the way in this kind of regulated assistance. We could learn a lot from his achievements in that field.

Afterwards they could go to university a much more rounded and mature person and get their degree over a much shorter period. Or they could go to college and study a useful course, or attend a place where they could acquire skills in the various trades.

There should be a full enquiry into the best way forward for further education. The enquiry should be manned not merely by government "experts" who have their own axes to grind. Instead it should be manned by retired persons from trades, occupations and professions with a good working record. They will also come a good deal cheaper, as many skilled retired people are only too eager to use their expertise to the advantage of future generations. After all, most of us are parents or grandparents or both. Retired persons now live long lives but are just dying to be able to contribute usefully to the welfare of the young and their country in general. The wisdom and knowledge of experienced, mature, skilled, gifted, down-to-earth pensioners is being wasted.

The Gospel according to Harry realises it is very easy to generalise. As George Bernard Shaw so aptly put it, "The trouble with youth is that it is wasted on the young". Very true. How often have we oldies said, "if I'd only known that before". But nevertheless we have to provide a basic structure of upbringing and education and this needs urgent attention.

One of the problems of Britain, however, is an attitude which is too often negative and sometimes rooted in deep cynicism. We simply need more optimism, more of a can-do attitude. People who say politicians are all the same, what's the use, are quite simply opting out, they are virtually saying nothing can be done. Wrong. Many politicians and public officials are very sincere and hard-working. Those who aren't should be chivvied. But they cannot do everything.

The Gospel of Harry says that people must be less apathetic and more public-spirited. Their country is going rapidly down hill. What can you do to stop the decline? It is not enough just to put 10p in a collecting box. Enthusiasm and application are required.

6

Britain today

I came into this world six and a half years after the end of the bloodiest conflict the world has ever experienced. The map of the world at that time was generously shaded with red, signifying that those countries "belonged" to Britain. Under the Crown we influenced the great dominions of Canada, Australia, New Zealand and South Africa. The vast sub-continent of India and what is now India, Pakistan and Bangladesh were subject to British rule. So also were many of the Caribbean Islands, the Malay States, Singapore and many other smaller countries. Five years after I was born there came the Wall Street Crash and the Great Depression.

Britain had pioneered industrial development. Britain had led the world in the cotton and iron and steel trades, mining, the development of railways, and we still ruled the mighty British Empire. And yet the great majority of British people lived in poverty or near poverty.

In 1935 the tyrannical Nazi regime came into power and by 1939 the world was engaged in another destructive six-year war. At the end of the war not only were the people in dire straits but the government was also broke.

But the British people worked hard and gradually standards improved. Due to the advance of technology, ordinary people were able to own telephones, refrigerators, central heating, washing machines and motor cars. People who hanker after the "old days" forget that they were only able to have a hot bath once a week, a change of shirt and underwear perhaps twice a week. Instead of a clean shirt you might just qualify for a clean collar as most shirts were made with detachable collars. Do you older men remember those lovely stud marks we had on the Adam's apple?

Overseas holidays were reserved for the very well-off, for the rest of us it was a week in rainy Blackpool or in showery Brighton.

Before the advent of plastic cards, if you wanted a washing machine or a television set the average family had to put down a deposit and pay it off on the "never-never". No instant unmanageable debt which is presently blighting the nation. So in 1962 our Prime Minister, Harold MacMillan, was able to boast to the nation with some justification that "You've never had it so good".

At the same time our Mr MacMillan was also talking about "the Wind of Change" in Africa. The government embarked on a programme of granting independence to their colonial possessions. India, "the Jewel in the Crown", had already been granted independence shortly after the war. Over a period of 25 years Britain shed its authority over the vast majority of its possessions. Nobody could really quarrel with that, the time for imperialism was over.

Many people in this country, including many in high places, still nourish a sense of guilt over Britain's part in "exploiting" the citizens of the Empire. They have no need to feel guilt at all. On balance the British Empire did more good than harm to its subjects. In any case, in the early days of Empire, everybody was exploiting everybody if the opportunity arose. It was the strong against the weak. The inhabitants of the world were strongly influenced by their blob instincts. But the British had a greater sense of fair play, particularly when compared with the Spanish Empire who simply annihilated the native populations of the Aztecs and of the Canary Islands. The French and Belgians also had a cruel record in colonisation. The main exploitation of Indians was carried out by other Indians rather than their colonial masters. To this very day the Indian people are influenced by a rigid caste system. We don't hear very much about "the Untouchables" nowadays but they still exist in large numbers. Africans and Arabs were as much involved in the start and maintenance of the slave trade as were the British and the Americans. Consider too the former state of Rhodesia which was made prosperous by British efforts. Now known as Zimbabwe, it has been brought to its knees by the pitiful and pitiless Mugabe. Many other African countries and nations such as Burma are despotic and corrupt. As a result, many former colonial subjects are desperate to come to this country. Indeed, many of them are already here. If every government in the world had to "apologise" for its past misdemeanours we would be all constantly grovelling on our knees.

Let us, rather, look to our future. Unfortunately, this has been seriously jeopardised by events of the last sixty years. After 1945 the French and German governments embarked on a period of reconciliation. This was good because for the previous hundred years, aided and abetted by other European states including Britain, they had systematically been murdering each other. They began to investigate how they might now help each other by a series of Trade Agreements.

In 1958 a series of treaties establishing a "Common Market" was agreed by France, Germany, the Netherlands and Luxembourg. On January 1st 1973 a majority of the British people voted in a referendum that we should join the European Economic Community, or the Common Market as it was better known. At the time most British people were under the impression that we were joining some kind of trade agreement. We were soon to find out there was a group of European politicians hell-bent on forming the United States of Europe. They are at present three quarters of the way towards their objective.

Since 1973, we have been regularly handing over our authority to make laws to an Organisation now known as the European Union. This body is unelected, wasteful, harmful and corrupt. Would you, for instance, use a bank which has not had its annual accounts cleared by an auditing authority? Yet the EU has not had its accounts cleared for fifteen years. One year we witnessed the farce of the European Commissioners having to resign en masse only to be re-appointed the following week.

There are splendid, expensive buildings which have been constructed in Strasbourg to house the European parliament. Their function remains a mystery to the vast majority of the British public, but the best I can gather is that it is an advisory service only and has no legislative powers. My best advice to them is to disband and go home. The amount of money saved would be vast. The only thing they have achieved is bringing a whole new meaning to the term "expenses". The European Court of Justice with its often bizarre judgements should also be abandoned.

When I served in the Royal Navy the great fear was that you might be drafted to a big ship, like a battleship or aircraft carrier, rather than a destroyer, frigate or corvette. The reason was that on a big ship, the leadership was remote, the administration was soulless, the spirit was resentful. On a small ship with the right leader the result was the opposite. Every crew member had a sense of belonging.

Likewise, the whole European concept is simply too large and clumsy. The USA works because they have a common language and a common history. Also the individual States are very protective of their rights.

The Gospel of Harry says that small governments are more accountable and more effective. Citizens of the UK who are against membership of the EU are scathingly referred to as "Little Englanders". Well, England, and Britain for that matter, are little. But that hasn't stopped us from looking outwards over the past five hundred years. We should have no illusions about being a great power any more. But unlike the former colonies which are now independent nations, Britain should also be an independent sovereign nation. We are all citizens of the world, we are all members of the human race. The only higher authority we should recognise is the United Nations. The Gospel of Harry will pronounce on that disappointing organisation later...

Simultaneously with the loss of our thousand-year-old facility to make our own laws and manage our own affairs, successions of British governments have stealthily approved the foundation of what they like to call a multi-cultural society. To me there is only one culture. That is to further the advancement of the civilisation process, by means of enlightenment, technical and scientific advances, education, toleration, the arts, the right of free speech, just laws, consideration for others, and the application of our knowledge for the greater good.

For over a thousand years a great deal of strife and misery has been caused by our flawed and mediaeval Christian beliefs, which I am pleased to say are now being abandoned in droves by the British people. The Church of England is now a much diminished organisation and is now relatively harmless...

On the other hand, the Roman Catholic Church is in many ways not a force for good. Their insistence on banning the use of birth control has caused great poverty to people with large families. In fact there should be a global policy on birth control, as the earth is is fast becoming over-populated. Roman Catholic opposition to contraception has also resulted in the growth of the AIDS epidemic in Africa. Their opposition to the development of stem cells to find a cure for such diseases as Alzheimer's and Parkinson's are extremely misguided and unhelpful, particularly for those unfortunate people who suffer from those terrible diseases. There is nothing sacred in a human cell. A human male can produce five million sperm cells in one ejaculation, give or take a few thousand.

In the same way, the development of genetically modified crops is claimed to be humans "playing god" or interfering with nature. In fact agriculturists have always cross-fertilised seeds to achieve improved yields. Mankind has always interfered with nature, sometimes to their detriment, but mainly to their benefit. If we hadn't interfered with nature, we would still be living in caves. It is ironic to note that a Senior British Cardinal who is currently leading the opposition to these advances is fitted with a Pacemaker.

The idea that immigration should be simply based on race or religion is patently absurd. If we need immigrants (which is doubtful as we already have five million of our own people unemployed or unemployable due to the abuse of our welfare system, a third-rate education system and bad parenting), then we should take only people with special qualifications.

If we really do need immigrants they should be admitted on the grounds of their ability to contribute to the wealth of the country by being proficient in a trade or a profession and also by the ability to speak English. The idea that immigrants add to the "culture" of the nation by their quaint religions or by their race is simply absurd. It is a kind of reversed racism. It may be unfashionable to say so but the majority of the British population feel like foreigners in their own country and politicians are too timid to acknowledge this simple fact.

The majority of people do not, either, wish to be part of a United States of Europe. That is why, in spite of promises to the contrary, the people of Britain were denied a vote on the Lisbon treaty. They were denied a referendum because the politicians knew the British people would vote against it. What is needed is a written British constitution which would prevent our politicians abrogating our laws and rights in favour of a treaty which is universally recognised to be a thinly-disguised constitution for the European Union.

Although the majority of religions are relatively harmless, the extremes of the Muslim religion are downright dangerous. They believe that they are the one true religion; anyone who isn't a Muslim is an infidel, a poor misguided worthless person. It has been estimated by the security services that there are an estimated 75,000 Muslims in this country who would wish this country harm. Their wish is to destroy British property and to indiscriminately kill British people. In fact they already achieved this on July 7th 2005 and followed this with an equally wicked but mercifully unsuccessful attempt only two weeks later. Several other plots have been fortunately foiled.

The Muslims brook no criticism of their religion. Salman Rushdie wrote a book: as a result a fatwah was issued against him. That is simply an order for him to be murdered. Because of their constant cowardly deeds and constant threats they are responsible for the country incurring massive extra security costs, not to mention great inconvenience to the population. Until they learn to be tolerant of other beliefs or non-beliefs they will always be a constant menace to the country. A sense of humour might help, too.

Much of the reasoning for this hostile behaviour is put down to the invasion of Iraq. The invasion of Iraq was justified by removal of the pitiless murdering despot Sadaam Hussein. Although the aftermath of the Iraq war was severely botched by the Americans at least they were rid of a cruel tyrant who indulged in mass murder of his people. But after five years this "one true religion" is rigidly divided into two warring sects. Muslim is still murdering Muslim to this very day.

It must not be forgotten either that the whole Muslim-Western conflict was exacerbated by Muslims attacking various American personnel and property, culminating in the cowardly attack on the Twin Towers in New York, long before the attack on Iraq. They are openly against the Western way of life. But their way of life simply brings poverty. Their oil wells have brought untold riches to some

Muslim countries but this is only shared by a privileged oligarchy.

Another absurdity is the European Union agreement that any citizen of the EU can up-sticks and work in any other European country. This has resulted in a huge influx of the new Eastern European members pouring into our country. I am not blaming them personally, they only wish to better themselves and many of them are good workers. But this has resulted on a strain on our health, education and housing services. There are schools around the country where up to fifty different languages are spoken. Some people say that is a cause for rejoicing. But can you imagine a teacher having to cope with that? There should be immediate, urgent approaches to the EU to put this situation on hold. Surely laws or agreements can be modified if they prove disastrous. In fact, the government was offered a seven-year restriction on immigration from Poland but our wonderful government turned it down.

Britain is a small, overcrowded nation. It is now also inhabited by an unknown quantity of illegal immigrants. Instead of interfering with the education and health services our government should have spent some money on guarding our borders. Before we take in any more migrants we should get rid of all the illegal immigrants and get all the unemployed back to work. We should concentrate on instilling proper discipline in our classes and in our homes so that our young people are fitted to accept their responsibilities. There is also a lost generation of older people who are feckless and irresponsible.

When I was born, the British Empire was at its pomp. When I was sixteen I joined the Home Guard. I had a rifle put in my hands and was instructed to kill any invaders.

Hitler must have been trembling in his boots. Now the country is inundated with foreigners. Many of these have integrated with the British way of life and have contributed to our economy and social life. Most of them haven't. In any case, the British are a reserved people and they find it difficult enough to integrate with each other unless they are intoxicated. The Liverpool people despise Mancunians and vice versa. The citizens of Glasgow and Edinburgh have a mutual antipathy. The North despises the South as effete wasters, whilst people from the South regard the inhabitants of the North as primitive savages. The Welsh and the Scottish cannot abide the English who are indifferently unaware of this hostility. What we should strive for is to be rid of our blobbish tribal instincts and start respecting each other for our qualities.

In my lifetime we have been reduced from a major power in the world, something I do not regret. But today our country is full of strangers who do not even speak the language. We are governed largely by an unelected group of Europeans, so-called Commissioners whose administration is so corrupt they cannot even get the books passed by an auditor. Such a state of affairs would not be accepted by the members of a tennis club. Although I have no statistical evidence to support this I contend that the majority of people who live in this country agree with what I have written in this paragraph.

Unfortunately I have no fear of contradiction of this belief because a sinister faction has introduced itself into our society, something called Political Correctness. That phrase initially sounds good. We should all like our political decisions to be correct. But a more accurate description of PC as it is now known might be Prohibited

Conversations. This insidious indoctrination is designed not to offend the Bleeding Hearts Brigade, which claims a monopoly of wisdom on all things humanitarian. So the result is that the average, tolerant British person is discouraged from expressing his honest beliefs for fear of being vilified as a Racist or Little Englander.

There are several other versions which the letters PC bring to mind. How about Pallid Concepts, Pandora's Chest, Pitiful Comments or… well, I'm sure you can think of many others.

7

Uniting the Disunited Nations

The Gospel of Harry has spoken on the political situation and now wishes to pass judgement on the United Nations.

In between the two World Wars the League of Nations was formed. Its purpose was to maintain the peace between the nations of the world. It failed dismally. When the United Nations was formed in 1946, the lessons which led to the failure of the League of Nations should have been learned. They weren't. The United Nations is toothless and ineffective.

What is needed is a completely new constitution. The membership should be open to all sovereign members as it is now, but voting rights for each country should be graded on a points basis. Points would be awarded to countries on the basis of the following:

- They hold free elections at regular intervals.

- Freedom of speech is permitted for individual citizens and for Press and the media.

- They have a fair legal system which would forbid imprisonment or execution without trial. Torture of any kind would be forbidden.

- They must illustrate a proven concern for the environment.

- Freedom of religion or non-religion must be tolerated.

- An effective International Court of Justice should be set up with powers to enforce UN decisions.

Sovereign States would be awarded points on the basis of whether they uphold these provisions. The number of points held by a member would decide how many votes a country can cast on any one particular issue. In this way a full blown democracy would have more voting influence than some corrupt despotic dictatorship. Countries such as Burma and Zimbabwe would have no voting rights on this basis.

Most important of all, National armed forces for the purposes of National action should be abolished. Each country should provide armed forces in proportion to their population, but this force should be responsible to the United Nations. These services should be trained and based in countries other than their own. This provision would mean that an International force could deal with such cruel, ghastly, inhuman situations as those which have arisen in Zimbabwe and Darfur.

- Free trade should be applied to the whole world.

- All nuclear weapons should be abolished.

This sounds all too simple. That is because it is simple. Let us do it now! Britain and other members of the EU could achieve these objectives on a fraction of what they pay towards the massive wasteful European Union and the existing, equally corrupt and feeble, United Nations Organisation. With the necessary will, these provisions could be achieved in ten years. All that is needed is the will.

8

Kings, Queens and the British Constitution

The Gospel of Harry has spoken and now moves on to the Monarchy.

In a strange way, despite the illogicality of the monarchy in a democracy, it does work to a degree. This is partly because the British people have an affection for the present monarch and also a degree of affection for her successor, and indeed also his successor. But accidents could happen and we could end up with an idiot or a megalomaniac not sufficiently off-balance to be certified, succeeding to the throne. The monarchy nearly collapsed in the reign of Queen Victoria, who, devastated by grief at the death of her husband, became a recluse for over twenty years. It is a matter of pot luck.

There is also something very cringe-making about referring to another human being as "Your Majesty" whilst bowing or curtseying at the same time. And it isn't just the big boss, it is also all the relations. Your Royal Highness trips off the tongue quite easily in a period drama, but it sticks in the craw a little bit in reality. Then there follow the Dukes, Viscounts and Lords with their titles, Your Grace, My Lord, Your Ladyship, My Lady. Efforts to democratise titles, such as Sir Mick and Sir Alec are equally absurd and divisive. I recently saw a clip of a nauseating television show where a composer of musical theatre with a title was loftily deciding which young woman should play Nancy in a forthcoming production of "Oliver". "And now His Lordship will make his choice" says the announcer portentously. Ugh! Bad enough to have public auditions but to have some lordy lordy do it is the pits.

Likewise, the House of Lords is an anachronism. It has recently been stripped of much of its hereditary powers, but it still consists of unelected members. Yet in many ways we have to be grateful to them for turning down some of the more preposterous measures which have been passed by the Commons. That admission indicates that we need a second house to monitor legislation. But why do we have to call them Lords, for goodness sake, with all its deferential implications? Why can't they simply be called Senators or Representatives rather than Lordies or Ladies?

Whilst we argue about the EU constitution we would be better off writing a constitution for Britain in order to save it from further erosion of its powers. In my lifetime I have witnessed a succession of five monarchs. I remember the titles of George VI being reeled off on his accession, which took all of two minutes. They included Defender of the Faith (indefensible), Emperor of India and so on and so forth. Now the titles of a new monarch would be simply King (or Queen) of Great Britain and Northern Ireland and subject to the laws that Brussels sprouts.

There are factions who proclaim that the Royal Family should "modernise" if you'll pardon the use of that misused word. But how can you modernise an institution that is inherently archaic? If, having already stripped them of all their real powers, you were then to take away the palaces, ceremonies and trappings of power they would lose all credibility. Alpha males or alpha females or God-Kings or Queen-Goddesses have to have the lot. Kings and Queens don't ride in buses.

The Book of Harry is uncertain of the future for royalty. What is vital, however, is that we need a constitution desperately before we become a mere off-shore region of a European bureaucracy. In the meantime we should introduce emergency powers to insist any further European treaty must only be ratified by a referendum.

Any written constitution for Britain must recognise the likelihood of a break-up of the United Kingdom. The position with Scotland is particularly pressing. Their current government is only inches away from a Scottish National Party clear overall majority. It is also a very ironic situation in that Scottish revenue per head of population doled out by the UK government is higher than for the English population. So the Scottish Parliament is able to treat the Scots to free medication and free university education. The Welsh Assembly has also used its powers to provide free medication and other goodies. The final irony is that the executive of the UK government has a proportion of Scottish ministers out of all proportion to the UK population. These currently include the offices of Prime Minister, Chancellor of the Exchequer, Defence Secretary and a host of junior ministers. These Scottish ministers and Scottish Members of Parliament happily discuss English matters and make English laws which have nothing to do with them.

To misquote John Knox: Oh England, let us be rid of this Monstrous Regiment of Scotsmen.

I have a personal interest in this matter as I was born in Scotland of Scottish parents but was taken to live in Wales whilst only a baby. A succession of Scottish relatives constantly reminded me of my proud Scottish ancestry, whilst Welsh children taunted me because of my English accent. Although I have spent half my life in Wales, I received my secondary education in England. I feel British, but if I had to choose, I would say I feel more comfortable being English - but I'm not fanatical about it, unlike my Scottish grandmother whom I did not meet until I was eighteen. Her introductory words to me were "Harry, my boy, never trust the Sassenachs". I replied along the lines that they're not too bad and politely enquired if she had ever been to England, to which she replied: "No and I dinna want to go there neither."

I recognise that the Welsh and the Scottish people have a fierce pride in their Celticness. Indeed some Celts are almost professional Welshman or professional Scotsmen. It is simply enough merely to be Welsh or Scottish. But the ill-conceived so-called evolutionary process which brought a degree of self-government is unsatisfactory. We all have to learn that we cannot have our cake and eat it.

English people have been quietly resigned to being considered the ogres, the suppressors, the conquerors, the exploiters and all that nonsense. They see no reason to proclaim their Englishness. They are, in the main, just quietly grateful for being English. But wasn't the Act of Union in 1707 agreed peacefully and willingly by the Scottish and English Parliaments? Wasn't the Tudor dynasty formed by a Welshman, Henry Tudor? But this is history. If the Welsh and the Scottish require independence, let them vote for it.

But I sense a change. English people are now at last dimly beginning to realise that they perhaps are the exploited ones in the present situation, and they might do better on their own.

But please, not an English parliament, please, please not another layer of government.

There is another way. The Westminster parliamentary sittings could be divided between UK matters, where Scottish and Welsh members could attend and vote, and English domestic matters where only English members could attend. This matter should be resolved sooner than later.

As for the European Constitution, it is not wanted by the people of Europe, only by their politicians. England, or the component parts of Britain, should only be responsible to a reformed, effective United Nations.

When I started writing this book the economic situation was fairly rosy. Now it has become uncertain. Together with the uncertainty of environmental difficulties due to possible climate change, the times look ominous for future generations.

This only goes to emphasise the need for global solutions to global problems. The reformed United Nations must have real authority. National governments must be free, open and fair and should strive to advance the civilising process whilst recognising our basic, selfish motives.

9

The National Health Service

It would be more fitting, perhaps, if the above was called the National Ill-Health Service since its work concentrates on trying to correct ill-health rather than attempting to promote a healthy way of living. When I recently had to spend a short time in an NHS hospital, I was served toasted white bread for breakfast. Surely at least someone working in a hospital should know that white flour is denuded of the greater part of its nutritional value.

When I was very young I remember being given a very good piece of advice by a much respected old gentleman. It was that the medical and legal professions should only be consulted in the most dire and desperate situations. I am now in my ninth decade and am pleased to say that I have not troubled these honourable professions too much in my lifetime.

I have been fortunate, but I think an attitude of mind to one's health is important. I was the youngest of three brothers and our outlook was that if you dared to say you felt ill, you were considered a cissy. I remember my middle brother suffered constantly from asthma attacks, but he would seldom complain. He would only reluctantly come indoors on the specific instruction of a parent or an adult.

It is an unfortunate fact of life that many of us are born with, or develop, terrible illnesses and have to suffer debilitating conditions. These people need all the help and resources that we can muster. But for every one person like that there are several people, who at the slightest twinge or pain, go running after a doctor for a "cure". Their attitude is that for every little ailment there is a pill or remedy to cure us. In fact, most ailments heal themselves. The medical profession agrees that there is no cure for a common cold, but the chemist's shops bulge with so-called remedies for it. Many doctors are driven to despair by hypochondriacs who pester the life out of them for trivialities. Billions of pounds are wasted every year on unused medication which clutters up the cupboards of thousands of homes. Most of it isn't needed, in fact a lot of it is harmful.

About twenty years ago, doctors were prescribing sedatives such as Vallium to thousands of patients who complained of stress and anxiety. The relief was only temporary, and worse, patients became addicted to the sedatives and clinics had to be set up to help wean them off this so-called remedy.

The Gospel of Harry advises that no medicine should be taken lightly. Doctors often prescribe medicines simply because patients feel, quite wrongly, cheated that they have not been given a magic pill. Stress is part of our blob ancestry. It is part of us having to exist in a constant state of danger from other tribes or species, of not knowing where your next meal is coming from, or whether you have a safe place to sleep. A certain amount of stress is good for us. It teaches us that we have to meet deadlines. It reminds us that we must strive to provide for and nurture our young. But to deny that there are people with severe mental problems would be foolish.

But nature, whilst often cruel, can also be kind. Get up in the morning, hop up and down, get the blood circulating, get active. If one is physically impaired, get the mind working on a problem. The human brain is a marvellous mechanism, it never actually stops working even when we are asleep but it must be stretched and tested, otherwise it declines.

Some people punish their bodies with machines in gymnasiums, others go jogging for miles gasping for breath. If that's what they want - fine. This is not a fitness manual, I leave that to the experts, but I do know that you have to keep physically active. The motor car has discouraged us from walking and the computer has encouraged us to sit down for long periods gazing at a screen.

But there are simple things that can be done. Getting off a bus one stop earlier is a good idea. Simple exercises can be carried out on a mat, a few press ups and simple stomach exercises can be easily devised. No fancy, expensive equipment is needed. My wife Jean is a great dancer and we often start the day with a movement session to the music of Elvis Presley or someone equally stirring. (I hesitate to call my efforts dancing.)

To each his own, but keep moving, keep thinking.

Another important aspect of good health is diet. I understand we are second only to the USA in the obesity tables. One cannot fail to notice the increasing number of seriously overweight men and women and, alarmingly, some of our children are also showing signs of obesity.

Here again, the cause of this lies in our blob ancestry. In the early days of Man our lives were a continuous non-stop struggle to find enough food to eat in order to survive. Occasionally an excess of food might appear. This could happen when certain trees or bushes yielded their fruit. Or perhaps there could appear an excess immigration of a weaker species which could go on the menu. Then our ancestors would go into Gobble Mode. It's a bit like putting something aside for a rainy day. The process of evolution has designed our digestive systems so that in the event of a sudden shortage of food we are able to go without food for several days or even weeks.

In the modern developed world there is no need to gorge. Unless you are very unfortunate there is ample food to survive on a daily basis. But we still have the inherited genes which tell us, come on, the food's there, let's get it down us.

Additionally, there are new huge industries which are devoted to seducing our taste buds. Highly-trained enthusiastic chefs appear on the television with enticing recipes to tempt us to eat more. And there are a multitude of fine restaurants offering food from the far corners of the earth. Against this there are guilt-ridden grub lovers trying to cope with complicated diets and usually failing.

There is only one way to lose weight. Here it is: Eat less.

Drugs are now an important and widespread feature of too many lives. The only non-prescriptive drugs which I have used in my lifetime are nicotine and alcohol. I can tell you that I smoked cigarettes for many years, suffered agony in trying to "give up" and frequently endured the humiliation of failing to rid myself of the addiction. The key to success in stopping smoking is simple. You don't "give up"; this implies sacrifice or deprivation. You don't give up, you stop. By stopping, you quickly regain the full use of your lungs and the sense of wellbeing which you enjoyed when you were a non-smoker.

Most people start smoking at an immature age, usually in their teens. They are brain-washed into believing it's cool, it's the thing to do and it is an enjoyable experience, all of which is simply nonsense. They don't enjoy them, but they are determined to join the ranks of smokers because it's the thing to do. So they work hard to overcome the coughing, eye-watering effects in order to accustom their bodies to the poison. In a very short time they are hooked, often for life.

What happens is, when the nicotine leaves your body after those first few cigarettes, you feel uneasy and slightly on edge, so you light up again and you begin to feel like you felt as a non-smoker again. You will then foster the much-cherished illusion that cigarettes help you to handle stress. But the stress which you relieve is simply caused by the nicotine with which you are regularly dosing yourself, to the detriment of your health and your bank balance. So you have to break that sequence by looking forward to the benefits you will achieve when you stop smoking.

You won't cough, you might be able to run again, you won't stink, your clothes won't smell, you'll probably save £2000 per year, you won't be a slave to an addiction, you won't be a social leper, and above all you'll rid yourself of that terrible periodic sense of uneasiness which you didn't have when you were a non-smoker.

You never get a high from smoking. All the smoker is doing is continually replacing the nicotine, which quickly leaves the body, which in turn rids the smoker of that feeling of wellbeing which they had when they were a non-smoker. In fact, what a smoker is doing is trying to return to the state of wellbeing which he already enjoyed as a non-smoker. How daft can one get? Stub that fag out and start living again.

The tobacco industry is the greatest commercial confidence trick ever imposed on a gullible public. There are no advantages to be gained from smoking, only serious disadvantages. If you need help in stopping smoking I recommend Allen Carr's very helpful book on the subject. But nowadays our profligate NHS is freely prescribing cigarette substitutes such as nicotine patches, pills or gum. This is simply taking the poison by another method and can be equally addictive. It also pleases the tobacco industry as they make greater profits from the substitutes than the cigarettes. If you are a smoker, do yourself a big favour. Stop today.

Unlike smoking, when you take a glass of alcohol you do experience a "high". You undergo a sense of pleasure and a loosening of inhibitions. Unfortunately it is sad to say there exists almost a feeling of hostility towards those who do not take alcohol. It is a good idea to remind ourselves that feelings of pleasure and self-confidence can be achieved without taking alcohol and abstainers are to be admired rather than despised. You don't actually need alcohol to lead a full life.

But most of us are blemished blobs. So much of social life today is centred around wining and dining and it is very easy to fall into the alcohol trap. Fortunately alcohol, unlike nicotine, is not immediately addictive. It can take several years of heavy drinking before one descends into the dreaded alcoholism with its devastating effect on the individual and family.

On the whole, I think alcohol can be a good thing. It helps to break down barriers and it helps to put aside problems for a while. But we must beware. With increasing prosperity, consumption of alcohol has rocketed. There is much learned discussion about the varying quality of your tipple. Some of this is valid, I'm sure, some of it strikes me as being a little pretentious. Whilst so-called pundits like Michael Winner preposterously claim that they never drink a bottle of wine under £1000 per bottle, I think that most of us blobs drink to get that pleasant feeling, that little lift. But now it is becoming more frequent to go beyond that little lift and become deliberately plastered, bladdered, lardered or whatever current phrase one chooses to describe being very, very drunk.

Ask any policeman what he thinks of the Friday and Saturday night shift. They won't be volunteering. The town centres of Britain are virtually no-go areas for sober citizens. They are filled with staggering, squabbling, vomiting young people, not a pleasant sight. Surely there can be no enjoyment or sense in reaching that state.

But this is not a new phenomenon. We all remember the Hogarth prints where the less well-off citizens are graphically portrayed in their mindless intoxication. We have also seen paintings of our richer, pot-bellied great great grand-parents quaffing their tipple to excess. It is not just a British thing, the Russians have the edge on us but we can probably claim the silver medal for over-indulgence.

I think that today too many families have retreated to the television set or the computer. Many families only rarely share a meal together. Nowadays there are fewer live local events happening. We are losing our sense of fun, and the art of conversation is dwindling. Hence the need for the booze to loosen us up.

Sadly, too, that grand old institution the British pub is having a very difficult time. They depend mainly now on the sale of food for their living, so the days of going to the local for a couple of drinks and a friendly chat are disappearing. Consequently, more people are drinking at home; it is also much cheaper.

But when we do get together for a night out, it's a binge. The British have always been notorious for "keeping themselves to themselves". The Americans and Australians are far more out-going. The British are too buttoned up. When the booze unbuttons us, we tend too often to go over the top.

It is humiliating to learn that the Football Authority controlling the 2008 European Football Cup decided that opposing fans in the competition need not be segregated only after the British teams had been eliminated in the preliminaries. The British also have a terrible reputation in overseas summer holiday resorts where they descend in their drunken hordes. The authorities in Spain and Greece in particular have been driven to distraction. It does not make you feel proud of your fellow-countrymen. We need to mature. I'm all for people having a fling, but there are limits.

10

Civic Pride

I do believe there is a simple solution for reducing the deterioration in bad behaviour and generally improving the quality of our lives.

The Gospel of Harry states that we need a return to Civic Pride.

I have always liked and participated in sport. But nowadays, we are too interested in one set of over-paid mercenaries recruited at huge expense defeating another similar group of spoiled, petulant ball-kickers. In professional football today it is a misnomer to talk about "your" team. You'll be lucky to find a British person in your team, let alone a local player.

Not so long ago, Yorkshire mothers-to-be living out of their county were coerced by their cricket-loving husbands to return to their county to give birth. This was to allow their child to qualify for the Yorkshire County Cricket team in later life. In my lifetime you had to be born in Yorkshire before you could play for their County. That is because Yorkshire men and women were proud of their Yorkshire heritage. I got more pleasure from my local Rugby team winning their league, rather than cheering on any band of cynical mercenaries. Why don't we return to having local pride in our town or city or village?

I have already referred to the lack of discipline in schools and how this could be dealt with. Now I am going to ask you three questions which I hope you will silently and honestly answer.

- Do you know the name of your local Councillor?

- Do you know the name of the Leader of your Council?

- Do you know the name of your local Chief Constable?

I suspect the answer is No. That is because they are anonymous.

One reason for this is that the Westminster government, having lost most of its powers to the European dictatorship, has taken away nearly all the power and authority from the local authority. They are merely puppets dancing to the tune of Westminster.

What is needed is this. Each local authority should have an elected well-paid mayor. We can afford to pay anonymous officials large salaries, let us pay it to someone who can be voted in or voted out. We have made a start in London. There is also a good case for a Chief Constable to be voted in or out. We should imitate a part of the French system of local government. Every authority in France has an elected Mayor. He is known by every citizen in the town and is the person who can initiate speedy action where required. If something goes wrong, such as some rowdies going beserk on our streets on a Friday or a Saturday night, we get hold of the Mayor, who will have a name and a reputation, a good one, hopefully. We can then request him (or her) to deal with the problem. He gets the police out of their police stations to take action. More important, they take steps to prevent it recurring again. There can be no buck-passing. Council tax payers should become more effusive, more aware. Local government elections are sad and boring affairs: that is because we, the voters, have allowed this state of affairs to develop.

It is no good the central government issuing decrees and instructions from afar.

Now we seem to have an epidemic of knife crime. These mainly juvenile offences such as knife crimes and pestering the life out of long-suffering residents should be dealt with at local level, and every law-abiding citizen should rally round and help. The present situation where ordinary people attempt to take action against criminals and are subsequently treated as criminals themselves is absolutely monstrous.

The police and the law-abiding citizens must be allowed to reclaim our streets again.

To return to alcohol, in my view the occasional excess is OK, but I believe that drinkers who have to get regularly "plastered" are unhappy or insecure or both. It is a good idea not to drink every day, if only to confirm that you can, if necessary, live without it. It may sound boring, but we should attempt to cultivate a feeling of *mens sana in corpore sano*, a sound mind in a sound body.

Most of the other dangerous non-prescriptive drugs were not readily available in my youth, so I was never tempted and so I have no direct experience of them. But you don't have to have been a user to realise that the effects of taking cocaine and heroin are extremely damaging and far-reaching. It is generally conceded that a large percentage of crime is caused by addicts in desperate need of money to feed their addiction. Here again, local people should be more involved and insistent that their areas should be cleared of drugs.

Surely there must be a better way of controlling the supply of these illicit drugs, both to the individual and to the dealer. I feel certain that a better degree of control would be achieved if we had more direct involvement with local authorities and police as outlined on my comments on alcohol. We desperately need our police to come out of their stations where they are confined to form-filling duties. We simply should not put up with easy access to drugs in our own patch. Many people know who these suppliers are. With more involvement from local people and police these dangerous people should be remorselessly weeded out.

There should be a separate department in every authority in a prominent place in the area where people can share information. Areas should be cleared of drugs street by street. We should nag the life out of people who indulge in drug-dealing until we are rid of it.

The present state of affairs is accepted too readily. This results in parents being in a constant state of worry about whether their children will be tempted. Our present obsession with paedophilia, which incidentally occurs mainly within families, should be replaced with a similar obsession about drug supplying and drug taking. Lives are being ruined. The woods are burning.

Surely, too, there must be a better way of guarding our borders from drug smugglers, and indeed from illegal immigrants. The names of the countries who supply drugs to Britain are already known to the authorities. Our government should be carrying out more vigorous action against these countries. If they were dropping bombs on us there would be an outcry. Polluting our country with highly addictive drugs is just as harmful. There is too much resigned acceptance of these situations by the British public. One of the pathetic things about drug-taking is that so-called celebrities, rock-stars (or noise-makers as I prefer to call many of them), are seldom charged for drug-taking even though they are featured daily in the news. This just sends out a message that it is all pretty cool. Consequently our prisons are full and fast becoming unmanageable.

Drug addicts who have committed crimes should be sent to separate prisons where all the efforts should be concentrated on their addiction. These could be provided by old vessels moored in harbours or anchored off-shore. A carefully supervised system could be devised where those convicted could be released as soon as they are pronounced "clean" and re-imprisoned if they are found to have become "users" again. The system should be managed in a spirit of more in sorrow than in anger.

We must be much more serious and vigilant about these crimes which are wrecking hundreds of lives, not only of the users but of the victims of their crimes.

But it would be much easier, of course, if each individual would say "No thank you, I am not having them".

So the Gospel of Harry, in its quest to seize the Moral High Ground, would simply say: do not use non-prescriptive drugs and use alcohol only as an occasional pleasure, not as a major prop to your way of life.

11

Hopes and Conclusions

The main thrust of the Gospel according to Harry is to claim that we are not sinful people who have to atone for our sins to a fictitious god. We must live for this world, not for some hoped-for paradise in an after-life. And that, I am certain, is the gospel truth.

We are, in fact, animals with basic instincts. This is not as bad as it sounds. Animals have good instincts to their fellow creatures as well as selfish ones. There are forces for good locked away in our genes somewhere and we must nurture those forces. We have come a long way from the brutish animals we were some 150,000 years ago. Mankind has committed terrible things in that time but let us remind ourselves of some of the great achievements we have made. In those years we have made great works of art, paintings, sculpture, beautiful buildings. Great works of literature have been written, magnificent music has been composed. We have made giant steps through the media of science, engineering and technology. We have cured many diseases. We have enabled persons to communicate with other persons at the far corners of the world at the touch of a button, we have made aircraft which circle the world in hours, made magnificent ships which sail the oceans.

Not least of our unheralded achievements, we have created sewage systems which made city life bearable and have rid the developed world of the dreaded cholera and other diseases. We are now on the fringe of space exploration. The doors are opening to all sorts of new discoveries, there is no end to what may be achieved.

We are now at the start of a revolution in the science of genetics. We already have the ability to create pest-free crops. Due to religious influences we are already behind most countries in this field. We must start thinking logically and close this gap as soon as possible. World scientists may soon be able to eliminate certain diseases by modifying the gene. We have made all these advances without the assistance of any god. They have all been made by intelligent, educated, clear-thinking, new-thinking men and women. But, of course, we must be careful that any scientific advance is to the advantage of the people. So we must be vigilant on these matters.

But we must never, never, never accuse our scientists of playing god. Scientists can only seek the truth. It is up to the Human Race to decide what is good for us, not some unknown fictitious entity.

If we waited for a non-existent god to help us we would still be living in caves. If we had lived "as Nature intended" we would never have built a hut or forged a tool.

But we blobs must also aim to create the Moral High Ground… or to put it more simply in common parlance just be good guys. Words like honesty, integrity, reliability, warmth and compassion for one's fellows spring to mind. The British Humanist Association is already leading the way in creating high moral standards without the need for religious faith. They should have greater recognition.

It is all in the upbringing. It is reckoned that the first five years in a child's life are the most important for character forming. This is when they will learn (or not learn) that they are a higher form of animal, the human animal. They will (hopefully) learn that the world does not revolve solely around them; their fellow humans must be considered. A parent must be loving, but firm. This applies to all classes of people, rich and poor alike. It isn't easy, but it is essential. Some people actually believe that children should never be criticised. It hurts their feelings. It shatters their confidence. A constant diet of praise will simply halt their progress. This is where some parents and teachers have failed recently and it is not an exaggeration to say we have lost a large part of a generation.

A good basis for training is the good old Boy Scouts and Girl Guide movements who indulge in all sorts of interesting and useful activities and are bound by sound principles of behaviour. Unfortunately, these movements may be seen as "uncool", the ultimate crime in the eyes of our youth. The oath should be altered, however, to swear to become a better citizen rather than to god and country. But many young people would rather sit around and gently moan about there being nothing to do.

There is always something useful and interesting to do.

Unfortunately we are now obsessed with paedophiles and it is sad to record that there are thousands of young girls and boys waiting to join these organisations who are unable to do so. The reason for this is that there is a long waiting list of adults waiting to help who have to be cleared by the police.

One Scoutmaster who had worked in the Scout Movement for many years ruefully confided in me: "You put hours of your time in, trying to help young people and although you enjoy doing it, everybody thinks you're a paedophile." What an attitude. Such people should be supported, not derided.

The most important part of our life is helping one's children, and other children too, onto the right track.

As a nation we have, in the main, unfortunately adopted a cynical attitude. A no-can-do attitude instead of a can-do outlook. A word that should be dropped from the English language is the word "cool" in the sense that being "cool" is the thing to be. Why don't we get a bit heated occasionally, more demanding, more eager to improve our society? Don't be cool, get warm occasionally.

It is too easy to say that politicians are all the same, they're just out for what they can get. This is just a cop-out to avoid the responsibility of having to think. There are many honest, hard-working politicians, often people who give up better paid jobs because they want to help. Of course, there are bad eggs in the basket. Where politicians are corrupt they should be weeded out and replaced.

It is known that the European Commissioner system has been proved to be corrupt and I also believe that the European Parliament, if not corrupt, is expensive and irrelevant and should be abolished immediately. What a saving that would be to the taxpayers of Europe. What a relief it would be to rid ourselves of those Champions of the Expense Account. There is a problem at the moment with expenses in the House of Commons and many people believe that members' salaries and expenses should be decided by an independent body. That project should be vigorously pursued.

But if we cannot trust our politicians we will descend into a corrupt, failed state, of which there are, unfortunately, many scattered around the world.

As I type this page in late September 2008, the world faces an unprecedented financial crisis which could result in the collapse of the structure of the civilised world. Remove our income, our ability to afford travel or our ability to feed ourselves and our families and we might be shocked to discover how quickly we revert to the primitive savagery of our blob ancestry.

I have tried to write this gospel in a light-hearted manner without pomposity. But the situation today is deadly serious.

We thought our banking system was safe. It wasn't. In simple terms, for the sake of greater profit, some banks have been lending money that is not covered by savings to people who have very little hope of repaying their debts. Worst of all, the reasonable debts are polluted with the bad debts. Because of the banks lending these bundles of mixed debts to each other, most banks do not know how many bad debts they are responsible for.

This is simply our blob background destroying what for many years have proved to have solid foundations. Because of greed this foundation has crumbled.

The Gospel According to Harry does not claim to have much in the way of original ideas. It is simply trying to state what the majority of the citizens in this country believe. That our standards and institutions have declined. This decline must be halted.

When I started writing this book, I was only stating improvements which were desirable. Today I consider them to be essential.

But we must remain optimistic. The human animal has a powerful brain and is resourceful.

It would be patronising and arrogant for me to produce a great list of Dos and Don'ts.

But, as our teachers used to put on our school reports: We must do better.

Never be bored. Keep asking questions. That way you may find useful answers.

Have a good life, be a good, kind, civilised animal.

Best wishes from

THE GOSPEL ACCORDING TO HARRY.

Amen.